"This book is essential reading for capability scholars. With remarkable depth and clarity, it traces the roots and implications of Amartya Sen's motivational pluralism, drawing us into a rich and wide-ranging conversation that spans from classical thinkers, such as Aristotle and Adam Smith, to contemporary voices such as Harsanyi, Ricoeur and Davis. At its heart, this is a compelling intellectual journey: from the narrow confines of self-interested and self-regarding behaviour that dominate mainstream economics, towards the broader horizons opened up by commitment, self-sacrifice, social embeddedness and mutuality, not coincidentally, the very foundations of the civil economy tradition. Yet this is far more than a work in the history of ideas. It speaks directly to one of the most unsettling issues of our time: the motives that drive our decisions, illuminating the rise of social enterprises and the search for alternative economic paradigms, including the bold vision put forward by the Economy of Francesco. Beautifully argued and intellectually generous, this book is an achievement to be celebrated: it enriches both scholarship and our collective imagination of what economics could and should be".

Flavio Comim, *Dean IQS School of Management and Full Professor at Universitat Ramon Llull-Barcelona, Elected Member of the "Human Development and Capability Association" and Research Associate at the "Von Hügel Institute" at Saint Edmund's College-Cambridge*

"The widely recognized exhaustion of the neoclassical research program has created greater openness to alternative research agendas and renewed interest in the work of influential economists such as Amartya Sen, whose contributions have been substantially marginalized because they do not fit neatly within the neoclassical framework. Valentina Erasmo's book offers an ambitious and original contribution to the development of these emerging research programs. Adopting an interdisciplinary perspective, it demonstrates how civil and social issues can be effectively examined through the theoretical lens of Sen's economic agents and economic motives. A book which deserves to be widely discussed".

Roberto Marchionatti, *Professor Emeritus at the University of Turin and Member of the Scientific Committee of the "Fondazione Luigi Einaudi"*

"A veritable *tour de force* that sets out Amartya Sen's understanding of individual behavior (based on social commitments and self-sacrifice), contrasts it with homo economicus, and derives its policy implications".

Steven Pressman, *Professor Emeritus at Monmouth University and Part-time Professor at the New School for Social Research-New York, Former President of the "Association for Social Economics"*

Economic Agents and Economic Motives

Economics has long been shaped by the figure of the self-interested individual. Yet many forms of economic action cannot be adequately understood through the lens of self-interest alone.

This book reconstructs Amartya Sen's understanding of economic agents and economic motives, showing how concepts such as commitment, self-sacrifice, agency, responsibility, and capabilities contribute to an alternative view of economic behavior grounded in social relationships. Drawing on the history of economic thought, economic methodology, and social economics, the book situates Sen's reflections within a broader intellectual tradition that includes Aristotle, Adam Smith, and the civil economy tradition. It argues that Sen developed an implicit but coherent conception of economic agents as socially embedded individuals whose decisions are shaped not only by personal advantage but also by ethical commitments, concern for others, and participation in collective life. The book further explores the strengths and limitations of this perspective through a dialogue with contemporary interpretations of Sen's work and examines its relevance for understanding hybrid organizations, particularly social enterprises. By connecting Sen's ideas to questions of reciprocity, cooperation, and social responsibility, it offers a novel framework for analysing economic action beyond the conventional model of *homo oeconomicus*.

This book will be of interest to scholars and students of social economics, the history of economic thought, economic methodology, political economy, and capability studies. By bringing together historical reconstruction, methodological inquiry, and contemporary socioeconomic challenges, it also offers valuable insights for researchers working in applied and qualitative economics, social enterprise studies, and related fields concerned with the social and relational foundations of economic action.

Valentina Erasmo is an affiliated researcher at the University of Turin and a member of the Executive Committee of the History of Economics Society. She previously held postdoctoral research positions at the University of Chieti-Pescara "G. d'Annunzio", the "Economy of Francesco Academy", the University of Turin, and the University of Bari. Her research focuses on the capability approach, the history of economic thought, and economic methodology, with particular attention to their qualitative applications to contemporary economic and social issues, including social enterprises, pluralism in economics, and civil economy.

Routledge Advances in Social Economics

Series Editor: John B. Davis, Marquette University

This series presents new advances and developments in social economics thinking on a variety of subjects that concern the link between social values and economics. Need, justice and equity, gender, cooperation, work poverty, the environment, class, institutions, public policy and methodology are some of the most important themes. Among the orientations of the authors are social economist, institutionalist, humanist, solidarist, cooperatist, radical and Marxist, feminist, post-Keynesian, behaviouralist, and environmentalist. The series offers new contributions from today's most foremost thinkers on the social character of the economy.

Publishes in conjunction with the Association of Social Economics.

Virtues, Morals and Markets
Why Moral Identity Matters
Rojhat Avsar

Political Economy, Institutions and Virtue
Alasdair MacIntyre's revolutionary Aristotelianism
Matías Petersen

Normative Economics in the History of Economic Thought
Marx, Mises, Friedman and Popper
Sina Badiei

Economics of Social Relations
Critical Perspectives on Social Capital
Atilano Pena López and Matías Membiela-Pollán

Economic and Social Welfare
A Cultural Approach
William A. Jackson

For more information about this series, please visit: www.routledge.com/Routledge-Advances-in-Social-Economics/book-series/SE0071

Economic Agents and Economic Motives

From Amartya Sen to Social Enterprises

Valentina Erasmo

Routledge
Taylor & Francis Group
LONDON AND NEW YORK

First published 2027
by Routledge
4 Park Square, Milton Park, Abingdon, Oxon OX14 4RN

and by Routledge
605 Third Avenue, New York, NY 10158

Routledge is an imprint of the Taylor & Francis Group, an informa business

British Library Cataloguing-in-Publication Data
A catalogue record for this book is available from the British Library

ISBN: 978-1-032-46314-8 (hbk)
ISBN: 978-1-032-46315-5 (pbk)
ISBN: 978-1-003-38109-9 (ebk)

DOI: 10.4324/9781003381099

Typeset in Times New Roman
by KnowledgeWorks Global Ltd.

To my parents, and to all my loved ones

Contents

Acknowledgement

Writing this book has not been easy. The academic world often encourages us to display optimism about how easy it is to achieve our results. However, before being economic agents, we are human beings. Complexity and difficulties are part of every researcher's life, and there is no shame in acknowledging the obstacles encountered along the way. Motives are often not enough to act. It has been a long journey, with its ups and its downs, one that led me to reflect on topics I had already explored in my previous research while discovering new ones, with the hope of offering readers an original and engaging book. And yet, here we are, at the point of seeing this book in print because will is often stronger than unexpected events and uncertainty.

Along this journey, I have been extremely lucky to count on two people in particular: on the one hand, Andy Humphries, who suggested turning my working paper – awarded the *Association for Heterodox Economics 2021 Best Early Career Research Prize* – into a book, guiding me patiently and expertly through every stage of the editorial process; on the other hand, John Bryan Davis, whom I consider my mentor, for his constant feedbacks on this and other works, as well as for inspiring me with his distinctive enthusiasm and passion for interdisciplinary research.

Alongside these two figures who accompanied me on this journey, there have been many others, all connected to the academic world, who contributed, directly or indirectly, to the realization of this work over the years. It does not matter whether they provided broad methodological insights, commented on an entire chapter, suggested references to strengthen my argument, or simply encouraged me with a kind word or a smile. I would like to thank them all, indiscriminately, with the same gratitude a scholar feels towards those who have built the foundation of their existence around their job. Thanks to, in strictly alphabetical order, Stefania Achella, Luca Alici, Angela Ambrosino, Angela Stefania Bergantino, Andrea Borsato, Carlo Borzaga, Luigino Bruni, Mario Cedrini, Enrica Chiappero Martinetti, the whole "Economy of Francesco" community, Luca Fiorito, Muriel Gilardone, Bill Gerrard, Mario Intini, Paul Lewis, Giorgia Lucchini, Roberto Marchionatti, Alain Marciano, Matteo Migheli, Simone Misiani, Gianluca Monturano (who supported me far beyond academic assistance), Manuela Mosca, Diletta Pasqualotto and the other coordinators of the Economy of Francesco village "Women for Economy", Steven Pressman, Scott Scheall, Paolo Santori, Piergiacomo Severini, Massimiliano Vatiero, Benoit Walraevens, and Carlo Zappia. I have also benefited from individuals I cannot name, including anonymous referees of my work, and participants at various seminars and conferences at which I have made presentations.

I would also like to thank some institutions also for their financial support: the European Society for the History of Economic Thought (ESHET) for awarding me the "ESHET 2023 Research Grant" for innovative projects presented by young scholars, which helped support the realization of this book; the "Economy of Francesco Academy" for funding me with a 2024 fellowship for research that contributed to this book; and the Department of Economics and Statistics "Cognetti de Martiis" at the University of Turin for supporting my research fellowship in 2024 and 2025, during which this book was completed

Last but not least, a special note of thanks goes to my family, my mother Laura and my father Ascanio, who have been and will continue to be present before, during, and after the writing and publication of this book, and to my four-legged friends in particular, Lilybeth whose companionship has brought joy and comfort throughout this journey.

Foreword

John B. Davis

Valentina Erasmo's *Economic Agents and Economic Motives: From Amartya Sen to Social Enterprises* breaks new ground in Sen scholarship and the explanation of human motivation in economic life. Sen, a Nobel laureate, of course made many original contributions to economics, and many have written about them. A young scholar might then wonder whether they ought to take on writing about Sen's ideas. But Valentina Erasmo has done this most impressively, and done so in connection with some of Sen's most fundamental ideas, thus herself making original contributions to the subjects Sen addressed.

Sen is best known for his thinking about capabilities, which has helped frame our understanding of the relationship between poverty and freedom and led to construction of the influential UN Human Development Index. Underlying this was his philosophical thinking about people's different types of motivations, his reflections on the impartial spectator idea, his influential thoughts about the concept of commitment, his reappraisal of the relationship between ethics and economics, and his emphasis on freedom and individual agency.

Erasmo's book begins with a review of the evolution of economic agents from the premodern thinking of the ancients to Adam Smith to the present and uses this to lay out what Sen added in his socially embedded impartial spectator conception. This provides her a window into Sen's key concepts of sympathy and commitment. But rather than simply repeat what has already been said on this, she explores self-sacrifice as a further, little recognized motive in Sen's thinking.

Sympathy and commitment are generally understood to be alternatives to self-interested behavior, but she argues self-sacrifice may also accompany them and act as a distinct type of motivation shaping people's behavior. Self-sacrifice, while often thought to be the most admirable sort of motive, is more complex than many appreciate. Sen's thinking on this developed under the influence of debates in the 1980s and 1990s when it was argued that gender norms in many societies cause women to accept personal deprivations and social disadvantages that lower their individual well-being. Women making self-sacrificing commitments to others may be the product of their own acceptance and others' promotion of exploitive social norms which limit their capability development. Thus, self-sacrifice to others might sometimes be better set aside and women act in their own self-interest. But how do they then still fulfill their commitments to others? Erasmo nicely brings out this complex issue in Sen's later thinking about the concept of commitment, demonstrating that people's social embeddedness creates tensions between responsibility and exploitation when excessive commitment leads to self-sacrifice.

Erasmo then goes on to open up new ground in her discussion of a little appreciated (indirect) exchange regarding agency, commitment, and social capabilities between Sen and the influential French philosopher Paul Ricoeur. Her focus is Ricoeur's emphasis on the idea of mutual recognition. Whereas thinking about the impartial spectator is generally framed in terms of how one imagines one is seen in the eyes of others, mutual recognition for Ricoeur involves others and oneself actively both recognizing one other. This adds a further dimension to how we think about Sen's concept of commitment. One's commitments to others may also reflect and depend on their mutual commitments to oneself, particularly when they live in the same communities. Erasmo's discussion of the Sen-Ricoeur exchange thus again adds another social embeddedness perspective to the interpretation of Sen's concepts.

This is all valuable, then, for how we think about promoting human capability development. In policy terms, this is often associated with the well-being of large populations of people, as in the UN Human Development Index. Yet on the smaller scale of communities where people interact and live, and where at the same time social discrimination and injustice commonly exist, mutual recognition provides a further condition and social basis for Sen's thinking about commitment and capabilities. Thus, in her closing chapter Erasmo takes this up in her application of Sen's capability thinking to social enterprises. Social enterprises are community-level, hybrid civil society economic organizations that balance profits and social goals in complex ways. They often depend on groups of people mutually recognizing one another's different needs and interests, and then drawing on this to cooperate economically in ethically motivated ways.

Much has been written about social enterprises, especially by scholars and activists in the long Italian civil economy tradition, but few have used Sen's thinking to explore its implications for individual communities. Connecting this literature to Sen and the capability movement is another demonstration of the originality and depth of Erasmo's thinking in this book. Pulling many ideas from the earlier chapters together, what she does in this chapter is show that a dualistic conception of person found in Sen's thinking about motivation combining individual agency and well-being provides foundations for a dualistic conception of social enterprises that similarly combines and serves these concerns for entire communities. Thus, Erasmo both opens up a new theoretical space for the capability approach and potentially extends an established applied policy literature to a new domain of everyday importance in the world today.

This book is highly informed by and knowledgeable of advanced literatures in the history of economics, philosophy of economics, and social economics. As such, it is an important contribution to those literatures. It is also a valuable contribution to thinking about community-level, applied social policy that should promote new empirical research stimulated by its insights. Valentina Erasmo has written an important book that calls for thoughtful reflection. We are fortunate to see it appear at this current time.

Introduction

0.1 The origins of this work

This work originates from my doctoral research conducted between 2017 and 2020. In those years, my research focused on Amartya Sen's conception of economic agents, particularly the period spanning the 1970s to the 1990s, when Sen introduced and further developed his well-known capability approach (Erasmo, 2019). My PhD dissertation offered a systematic investigation of Sen's understanding of economic agents and their leading economic motives, grounded in a joint historical and methodological perspective. Indeed, Sen elaborated his (largely implicit) view of economic agents during the same period in which he developed his capability approach, often in the very works in which he discussed its foundational elements.

In 2021, a working paper derived from my PhD thesis, entitled "Extending the capabilities conception of the individual in economics: relationality and responsibility" (Erasmo, 2025), was awarded as the best paper presented at the Annual Conference of the Association for Heterodox Economics (AHE). The AHE award marked the start of a larger project. Routledge subsequently invited me to develop a full-length book on the topic, expanding the original paper into a more comprehensive and systematic study. I am grateful to Andy Humphries and John Bryan Davis for the opportunity to further develop this project in a book for the Routledge Series *Advances in Social Economics*.

This book, *Economic Agents and Economic Motives: From Amartya Sen to Social Enterprises*, develops my early research on Sen while substantially extending it with new theoretical elements. Several chapters are entirely original contributions: for instance, the critical reconsideration of traditional conceptions of economic motives and agent behavior (Chapter 1), as well as the in-depth discussion of Sen's concepts of commitment and agency (Chapters 2 and 4). Other chapters, instead, those addressing self-sacrifice (Chapter 3), Sen's missing mutuality in social relationships (Chapter 5), and the analysis of social enterprises (SEs) through the distinguishing features of Sen's view of economic agents, develop insights from previous publications (Erasmo, 2021, 2022, 2023, 2025; Erasmo and Migheli, 2026). The book's general

DOI: 10.4324/9781003381099-1

theoretical framework is likewise rooted in ideas I have already developed in prior works, mainly those on the origins and development of the capability approach and its role in Sen's theory of justice and Sen's idea of the impartial spectator (Erasmo, 2019, 2024, 2026; Erasmo and Santori, 2025).

The *trait d'union* of these chapters is my interest in civil and social issues in economics. This sensitivity has deepened over the years of my academic training and postdoctoral research, thanks to the research groups I have joined. In particular, my view has been shaped by my involvement in the Economy of Francesco (EoF) Academy since 2021, whose Scientific Committee is directed by Luigino Bruni, as well as by my participation, since 2023, in the economic methodology research group of the University of Turin, led by Angela Ambrosino and Mario Aldo Cedrini, which focuses primarily on the relationship between economics and other social sciences. I am grateful to all the people behind these scientific (and human) communities for providing me with the tools to work on a highly interdisciplinary project like this.

In this book, all these ideas and influences are finally combined and extended with new insights around Sen's understanding of economic agents, also applied to SEs. In this way, this book contributes to a deeper understanding of how social and relational dimensions shape the behavior of economic agents, both individuals and firms. I will discuss the aims of this book and where my project sits in relation to the existing literature.

0.2 The aims of this book and a review of the literature

Although Amartya Sen was awarded the Nobel Prize in Economic Sciences for his studies on human development in 1998, he became widely known, above all, for his capability approach. This theoretical framework has profoundly reshaped how economists and philosophers think about human well-being, freedom, and social justice, offering an alternative to both utilitarianism and Rawls's theory of justice.

More specifically, Sen (1980) developed the capability approach as an alternative framework to utilitarianism and Rawls's theory. It is challenging to date the origins of the capability approach because the emergence of its key concepts, particularly functionings and capabilities, has been highly stratified over time (Erasmo, 2024). The concept of functionings, for instance, had been primarily introduced by the philosopher and economist Vivian C. Walsh (1961) through the term 'achievement' (Erasmo, 2019, 2026) when he was analysing the broader question of scarcity (Putnam, 2002).

If scarcity occurs "when anything needed for the achievement of an end (…) is insufficient for the end's attainment" (Walsh, 1961, p. 24), the concept of achievement is understood as the ability to pursue a chosen end for living a certain life. Subsequently, Amartya Sen (1985a; Sen and Dasgupta, 1983) further developed the concept of achievement in the context of development economics and renamed it "functioning", also introducing the notions of 'capability' and 'capability approach' (Sen, 1980, 1985a). Then, Martha C. Nussbaum (1992, 1999) wrote down a complete list of capabilities to make the capability approach more applicable to concrete economic (and non-economic) issues. In this way, the "capability approach" became a "capabilities approach". Thus, the origins and earlier development of the capability approach might be located between the Sixties and the Nineties.[1]

Among these works, however, one of the most famous is "Equality of What?" (1980), where Sen provided the first explicit formulation of what capabilities are. In this context, Sen (1980) argued that it is impossible to build a proper theory of equality based on the limitations of utilitarianism or Rawls's (1971) theory of justice. According to him, both theories have severe limitations. In this respect, utilitarianism "fails to capture the relevance of overall advantage for the requirements of equality" (Sen, 1980, p. 204). Instead, albeit Rawls's theory is interested in socioeconomic inequalities, his understanding of primary goods "leads to a partially blind morality (…) there is, in fact, an element of 'fetishism' (…)" because "Rawls takes primary goods as the embodiment of advantage, rather than taking advantage to be a relationship between persons and goods" (Sen, 1980, p. 216).

Based on their respective limits, Sen stressed that he wants "to present an alternative formulation of equality which seems to [him] to deserve a good deal more attention than it has received, and [he] shall not desist from doing some propaganda on its behalf" (Sen, 1980, p. 197), such as the capability approach. In a nutshell, Sen's approach focuses on human life, especially individual well-being and social states. The capability approach aims to explain "how to remove" those obstacles to expand capabilities for the largest possible number of people, thereby reducing socioeconomic inequalities (Erasmo, 2019). This purpose undoubtedly has social relevance and was shared by all those "capability scholars" named above. According to Sen (1985a), the concept of functioning refers to the achievement of a person, such as "what he or she manages to do or to be" in their existence, as well as "a part of the 'state' of that person". Still, it ought "to be distinguished from the commodities which are used to achieve those functionings" (p. 10). Instead, capability is about "those beings and doings that constitute human life and that are central to our understandings of ourselves as human beings" (Robeyns, 2017, p. 39).

More specifically, capabilities refer to the set of alternative functionings that represent individuals' freedom to choose between different combinations of functionings to improve their well-being. According to Sen (1985b), freedom means the 'freedom to' choose among different functionings, while capabilities refer to the freedom to lead a particular existence concretely. This possibility shows a positive correlation between expanding freedom and the opportunity to choose and achieve further capabilities and vice versa.

Thus, freedom equals the set of capabilities related to those functionings that can be chosen and exercised.

However, Sen refused to write down a complete list of capabilities: Among the reasons for this choice is the capability approach's incompleteness (Hédoin, 2016). Sen (1993) argued that we cannot practice a total comparison among two or more capability sets, but only a partial comparison among them, limited to those functionings that are considered meaningful everywhere and at any time. The impossibility of a total comparison arises from the heterogeneity and mutability of individual values and preferences. Based on this impossibility, Sen suggested limiting our comparison between two or more initial sets of functionings to obtain a partial but complete ordering of functionings, which can then be converted into capabilities. According to Sen (1993), this partial ordering corresponds to basic capabilities that might be desirable everywhere because they provide a preliminary condition for social well-being for all community members.

If Sen refused to write a complete list of capabilities, Nussbaum (1999) stressed the importance of introducing a list of well-defined capabilities based on her claim to clearly identify which are those "truly human functionings". The human capabilities she identified in her list are those of affiliation, bodily health, bodily integrity, emotions, life, other species, play, political and material control over the individual's own environment, practical reason, sense, imagination, and thought (Saigaran et al., 2015). These capabilities are distinct because they address separate components. So, these capabilities are independent in quantity but equally important in quality.

According to Nussbaum (1999), a list of capabilities should be introduced to take a stand for political purposes and provide an understanding of what a good life is for human beings. This "list is supposed to provide a focus for quality-of-life assessment and for political planning, and it aims to select capabilities that are of central importance, whatever else the person pursues" (Nussbaum, 1999, p. 53). For this purpose, Nussbaum's capabilities should be concretely specified in the light of local beliefs and circumstances, unlike Sen's capability approach, which primarily has heuristic value for promoting public reasoning about what is relevant to evaluating social states (Baujard and Gilardone, 2017).

Since the beginning of the 21st century, many works have analysed or extended the capability approach, but these interpretations are highly heterogeneous. For instance, Ballet et al. (2013), Bonvin and Farvaque (2016), Clare and Horn (2010), Davis (2012), Pressman and Summerfield (2002), Qizilbash (2007), Pressman and Summerfield (2002), and Robeyns and Brighouse (2010) suggested that the capability approach plays a key role in Sen's theory of justice (Baujard and Gilardone, 2017). Instead, Bénicourt (2007), Comim et al. (2008), Nussbaum (2003), Robeyns (2003), Shapiro (2011), and Sugden (1993) highlighted that Sen is probably not so interested in making his capability approach operative. Many scholars, like Alkire and Foster (2011), Comim et al. (2018),

Chiappero-Martinetti et al. (2020), Déneulin (2014), Déneulin and McGregor (2010), Gasper (2020), Kuklys (2004, 2005), and Robeyns (2017) applied the capability approach to human development, inequalities, poverty, and social justice, just to name a few. All these scholars primarily focused on Sen's capability approach, rather than other important ideas he developed throughout his long career. In a certain sense, these works contributed to the view of Sen as "a capability theorist" (Baujard and Gilardone, 2017).

However, some years ago, Sen interestingly stated: "I have to rescue myself by saying [thumping table] 'I'm not a capability theorist! For God's sake, I'm not a capability theorist'" (Sen in Baujard et al., 2010). In this way, Sen expressed his firm intention not to be regarded as a "capability theorist" urging scholars, on the one hand, to clarify the role of the capability approach within his broader theory of justice (Baujard and Gilardone, 2017; Erasmo, 2024) and, on the other, to consider aspects of his thought not directly connected to the capability approach, which may have been overlooked.

Halfway between these two possible lines of inquiry, the present work aims to highlight some concepts and ideas that Sen broadly discussed between the 1970s and the 1990s alongside the elaboration of the capability approach (for instance, agency, commitment, and self-sacrifice, but also responsibility, impartiality, and the dualistic conception of person in ethical calculus, to name just a few). Taken together, these concepts clearly suggest that, while formulating the capability approach as an alternative framework for exploring socioeconomic equality, Sen was also envisioning a different conception of economic agents and economic motives, distinct from the dominant paradigm of his time, namely the mainstream neoclassical *homo oeconomicus*, grounded in self-interest. It should be stressed that Sen never provided a systematic formulation of his conception of the individual in economics, despite offering all the necessary conceptual elements to reconstruct his perspective on this broad and complex topic.

The aim of this book is twofold. The primary goal is to reconstruct Sen's understanding of economic agents and their economic motives, evident throughout his works, even when not directly related to the capability approach. More specifically, this analysis reveals that Sen envisioned an alternative to the mainstream *homo oeconomicus* and social atomism, proposing a socially embedded view of individuals. The difference between social atomism and social embeddedness will be further explored below. Building on this rediscovered sociality in economics, this book also aims to demonstrate how Sen's understanding of economic agents and motives can serve as a theoretical foundation for the debate on hybrid firms, particularly SEs. These firms represent more-than-profit organizations that combine profits and social goals. The role SEs assign to sociality within firms brings them close to Sen's view of individuals, adopting commitment as the ideal economic motive in decision-making.

The emphasis on sociality explains the relevance of this topic for the *Routledge Series Advances in Social Economics*. Sen's conception of economic agents and economic motives places the social dimension at the very core of his economic anthropology. From a methodological perspective, this focus on sociality did not escape the attention of one of the most insightful interpreters of Amartya Sen's works, John Bryan Davis. In this respect, although Davis did not directly offered a historical reading of Sen's concepts related to economic agents, he nonetheless has the merit of being among the first scholars to recognize that Sen's capability approach could provide the theoretical foundations for rethinking the conception of individuals in economics beyond the social atomism of the neoclassical *homo oeconomicus*.

Building on Sen's insights, Davis (2003, 2009, 2024) proposed his own *capabilities-based conception of individuals* as socially embedded agents, thereby offering an alternative to the traditional, preference-based view that has dominated mainstream economics for decades. What are the distinguishing features of Davis's capabilities conception of the individual? Quoting his own words:

> A capabilities conception of the individual is a social conception of the individual. In contrast, then, to how the preferences conception of the individual explains individuals atomistically apart from society, a capabilities conception of the individual explains them in terms of social relationships.
>
> (Davis, 2009, p. 414)

According to the preference-based conception, economic agents are considered independent of one another by virtue of their "own" preferences. In mainstream economics, particularly among neoclassical economists, this assumption has made individual preferences the key basis for distinguishing one person from another. In this regard, neoclassical economists represented individuals "in terms of (…) 'well-defined preferences' that can be summarized by a single unique utility function" (Davis, 2003, p. 47). The neoclassical view generally treated economic agents atomistically in decision-making – that is, as autonomous in their individual goals and choices (Davis, 2011). This autonomy arises from agents' ability to limit themselves to their "own private concerns and objectives in a socially non-interactive manner" (Davis, 1992, p. 83) in order to maximize their welfare.

Probably the most well-known example of a preference-based conception of the individual is the early formulation of neoclassical *homo oeconomicus*, which perfectly embodies social atomism in economic behavior. However, the advent of the embedded conception of the individual in economics challenged both *homo oeconomicus* and social atomism beginning in the 1980s – the same years when Sen discussed the concepts that illuminate his own view of economic agents.

In general, the socially embedded conception of the individual has been most widespread within heterodox economics, where individuals are understood as situated within social and economic relationships (Archer, 1995; Folbre, 1994; Granovetter, 1985). Davis's conception of individuals in economics can be seen as one of these embedded approaches, due to the central role he assigns to sociality. In this respect, Davis suggested that:

> not only that heterodox economists ought to make capability analysis central to their understanding of individuals but that they ought to place special emphasis on that particular capability that individuals can acquire of being able to appraise their own positions across their continually changing social relationships. Whether individuals were to develop such a capability could be one focus of a specifically heterodox social economic policy.
>
> (Davis, 2009, p. 67)

Thus, individuals may evaluate and modify their condition in society through social relationships within economic dynamics, as will be illustrated with concrete examples below. Building on Davis's broad discussion, we acknowledge the intellectual debt this book owes to his ideas, as he was among the firsts to make explicit the role of sociality in Sen's thought through the capability approach. At the same time, we aim to emphasize the novelty of this work compared to existing literature, offering a unified interpretation of the concepts that allow us to reconstruct Sen's understanding of economic agents. In doing so, we show that a social view of individuals is already present in Sen's work, although it remains rather implicit in his discussion of economic motives.

Davis's conception of the individual and Sen's understanding of economic agents share a common foundation in social embeddedness. However, they differ in that Davis offers a new conception of the individual in economics, grounded in a methodological elaboration of Sen's capability approach, whereas this book makes explicit Sen's implicit view of economic agents also through their leading economic motives.

0.3 Some examples of how social relationships might improve individuals' condition within socioeconomic dynamics

Based on this theoretical background, the following examples illustrate how social relationships, as emphasized in Sen's and Davis's frameworks, concretely enhance individuals' socioeconomic conditions within different economic contexts. This exercise is important for understanding why sociality might be so useful in contemporary socioeconomic reality rather than social atomism. For instance, in SEs, the same firms we will explore in this book, decision-making is often participatory. Members collectively evaluate organizational policies, share information, and adjust their roles or contributions in response to mutual feedback. This embedded social structure enables individuals to enhance not only their own well-being but also the cooperative's overall functioning (Cornforth, 2004).

Other examples of how social relationships might improve individuals' condition in society through economic dynamics (Zamagni, 2021) include microfinance programs, community-supported agriculture (CSA), social learning in peer-to-peer networks, and participatory budgeting. In microfinance programs, for example, individuals' access to credit and their repayment behavior are influenced by their membership in social groups. For instance, Grameen Bank borrowers are organized into small solidarity groups, where members monitor and support one another. Through these social relationships, individuals can assess their economic positions, learn from peers' experiences, and adapt their strategies to improve financial outcomes (Armendáriz and Morduch, 2010). This example illustrates how economic exchanges are socially embedded (Granovetter, 1985), and how trust and reciprocity (two important dimensions of social capital) serve as substitutes for material collateral. In this sense, microfinance represents a form of economic action embedded in community ties, in line with the principles of the social economy, where cooperation and mutual support replace competition as the primary mechanisms of coordination (Defourny and Nyssens, 2017).

In CSA schemes, individuals participate in local food networks, investing labor or money upfront and sharing in the harvest. Through continuous social interactions with farmers and other community members, participants can learn about sustainable production practices, assess the impact of their consumption choices, and modify their behaviors to improve both personal nutrition and community resilience (Kneafsey et al., 2013). CSAs are what Laville (2010) identified as examples of "plural economy" where market exchanges are embedded within networks of reciprocity and ecological responsibility. These specific initiatives not only provide economic benefits but also foster social cohesion and a shared sense of stewardship towards local resources, aligning with the broader perspective of the solidarity economy (Laville, 2010).

Other possible examples of social relationships that can improve individuals' economic conditions include online or offline peer networks. They enable individuals to compare their outcomes with others', seek advice, and adopt more effective practices. For instance, in social entrepreneurship networks, members can evaluate the social and economic impact of their initiatives, adjust resource allocation, or innovate collectively. Similarly, in this case, social embeddedness influences individuals' ability to modify their circumstances (Senyard et al., 2014).

In the case of participatory budgeting (PB), instead, the improvement of individuals' socioeconomic well-being is directly linked to the quality and intensity of the social relationships built during the participatory process. Initially developed in Porto Alegre in the late 1980s, PB brings citizens together to discuss local priorities and decide how portions of municipal budgets should be spent (Baiocchi, 2005; Sintomer et al., 2012). These deliberative spaces create opportunities for interaction between diverse social groups, fostering trust, reciprocity, and collective problem-solving.

Through sustained participation, individuals strengthen their social capital – developing networks of support, learning negotiation and communication skills, and gaining access to information about public resources (Laville, 2010). This relational learning enhances people's capacity to influence local economic decisions and to access material and non-material benefits, such as improved infrastructure, community services, or employment opportunities generated by funded projects (Wampler, 2012). In a nutshell, social relationships play a central and constitutive role in the embedded conception of the individual, shaping both personal well-being and the collective dynamics of economic life.

0.4 Methodology and structure of the book

This book is primarily addressed to scholars in the fields of social economics, the history of economic thought, and economic methodology, as well as the capability approach scholars. However, its reflections may also be of interest to researchers and practitioners in the broader fields of philosophy and business organization studies. Its interdisciplinary character reflects the nature of the questions guiding the analysis: What does it mean to be an economic agent, whether an individual or a firm, in a socially embedded context? How can Sen's reflections on concepts such as commitment, self-sacrifice, and agency inform the current debate on hybrid organizations? In this sense, this book seeks to foster dialogue across disciplinary boundaries, inviting economists, philosophers, and social scientists to reconsider the socio-relational foundations of economic action. This conceptual framework highlights a latent affinity between Sen's economic thought and the distinguishing features of the social economy, such as the emphasis on reciprocity, cooperation, and ethical responsibility as constitutive dimensions of economic life.

This book is composed of six chapters, which together delineate a trajectory from the conceptual foundations of economic agents and motives to their institutional manifestations in a specific socially embedded organization, namely SEs. In particular, Chapter 1 provides an overview of the evolution of the idea of economic agents and economic motives from ancient philosophy to contemporary economics. Beginning with ancient philosophical thought, from Aristotle to the Pelagians, it examines how moral and civic concerns shaped early understandings of economic behavior. The analysis then moves through Scholastic thought and the civil economy tradition, concluding with Adam Smith and his impartial spectator between philosophy and economics.

Subsequently, Chapter 2 focuses on Sen's notion of *commitment* and the implications of this rational economic motive for redefining rational choice theory. By examining Smith and Harsanyi's joint influence on Sen's notion of commitment, the chapter introduces the notion of the embedded impartial spectator as one of the distinguishing features of Sen's understanding of economic agents.

Chapter 3 explores self-sacrifice as a further economic motive that broadens Sen's view of alternative economic motives beyond self-interest. This analysis reveals the ambivalent nature of self-sacrifice, balancing altruism with the risk of exploitation, and links it to gender inequalities, perception bias, and the fragility of strong social ties.

Then, Chapter 4 turns to the concepts of agency and capabilities, including the role of Sen's "goal rights system" for defining the moral basis for agency. Here, individuals emerge as moral agents in collective deliberation, promoting social well-being and rediscovering responsibility in economic decisions.

Chapter 5 presents an original reading of Sen's economic agents, as offered by the philosopher Paul Ricoeur, focusing on the notions of rights, recognition, and capabilities. It also shows Ricoeur's debt to Sen, as well as his criticism of Sen's failure to consider mutual recognition in social relationships, thereby highlighting the limits of Sen's view of economic agents. His sociality misses mutuality…or, probably not.

Chapter 6 examines SEs through Amartya Sen's view of economic agents, focusing on commitment, social embeddedness, and self-sacrifice. It traces the historical and conceptual roots of SEs, highlighting their blend of social and economic objectives. Using Sen's framework, the chapter analyses how altruistic motivation drives action while interacting with individual agency and capabilities. The chapter also addresses the limits of self-sacrifice (for instance, perception bias) and discusses possible strategies to raise self-consciousness among the most deprived people. Empirical examples illustrate how SEs navigate these dynamics, offering a nuanced perspective on their potential and constraints.

This book will end with some general conclusions on the issues addressed in the previous chapters.

Note

1 In "Equality of What?", Sen (1980) referred to capabilities in terms of "basic capabilities" as an informative basis about what a person is "able to do certain basic things" (p. 218), differing from other discussions about socioeconomic inequalities. Although the CA was born and grew between the Sixties and the Nineties, some of its distinguishing features (for instance, the criticism towards "commodity fetishism", the ideas of human flourishing and well-being) might already be found in scholars like Aristotle, Karl Marx, and Adam Smith (Robeyns and Byskov, 2020). For more about the history of the capability approach, see Erasmo (2024), but also Erasmo (2019) where I focused on the preliminary stratification of ideas that led Sen subsequently elaborate the capability approach between the Seventies and the Eighties.

References

Alkire, S. and Foster, J. (2011). "Counting and Multidimensional Poverty Measurement", *Journal of Public Economics*, 95 (7–8), 476–487. https://doi.org/10.1016/j.jpubeco.2010.11.006

Archer, M. (1995). *Realist Social Theory: The Morphogenetic Approach*, Cambridge: Cambridge University Press.

Armendáriz, B. and Morduch, J. (2010). *The Economics of Microfinance*, Cambridge: MIT Press.

Baiocchi, G. (2005). *Militants and Citizens: The Politics of Participatory Democracy in Porto Alegre*, Stanford: Stanford University Press.

Ballet, J., Bazin, D., Dubois, J. L. and Mahieu, F. R. (2013). *Freedom, Responsibility and Economics of the Person*, London: Routledge.

Baujard, A. , Gilardone, M. and Salles, M., 2010, A Conversation with Amartya Sen', *La Forge Numérique*, MRSH, Universitéde Caen Normandie (video interview). https://doi.org/10.60527/eae6-8085

Baujard, A. and Gilardone, M. (2017). "Sen Is Not a Capability Theorist", *Journal of Economic Methodology*, 24 (1), 1–19. https://doi.org/10.1080/1350178X.2016.1257821

Bénicourt, E. (2007). "Amartya Sen: un Bilan Critique", *Cahiers d'économie Politique*, 52 (1), 57–81. https://doi.org/10.3917/cep.052.0057

Bonvin, J. M. and Farvaque, N. (2016). *Amartya Sen: une politique de la liberté*, Michalon.

Chiappero-Martinetti, E., Osmani, S. and Qizilbash, M. (2020). *The Cambridge Handbook of Capability Approach*, Cambridge: Cambridge University Press.

Clare, J. and Horn, T. (2010). "Sen and Sensibility", *South African Journal of Philosophy*, 29 (2), 74–84. https://doi.org/10.4314/sajpem.v29i2.57050

Comim, F., Fennell, S. and Anand, P. B. (2018). *New Frontiers of the Capability Approach*, Cambridge: Cambridge University Press.

Comim, F., Qizilbash, M. and Alkire, S. (eds.). (2008). *The Capability Approach. Concepts, Measures and Applications*, Cambridge: Cambridge University Press. https://doi.org/10.1017/CBO9780511492587

Cornforth, C. (2004). "The Governance of Cooperatives and Mutual Associations: A Paradox Perspective", *Annals of Public and Cooperative Economics*, 75 (1), 11–32. https://doi.org/10.1111/j.1467-8292.2004.00241.x

Davis, J. B. (1992). "Atomism, Identity Criteria, and Impossibility Logic", *Methodus: Bulletin of the International Network for Economic Method*, 4 (1), 83–87.

Davis, J. B. (2003). *The Theory of Individual in Economics. Identity and Value*, London& New York: Routledge.

Davis, J. B. (2009). "The Capabilities Conception of the Individual", *Review of Social Economy*, LXVII (4), 413–429. https://doi.org/10.1080/00346760903254250

Davis, J. B. (2011). *Individuals and Identity in Economics*, Cambridge: Cambridge University Press.

Davis, J. B. (2012). "The Idea of Public Reasoning", *Journal of Economic Methodology*, 19 (2), 169–172. https://doi.org/10.1080/1350178X.2012.683596

Davis, J. B. (2024). *Identity, Capabilities, and Changing Economics*, Cambridge: Cambridge University Press. https://doi.org/10.1017/9781009438247

Defourny, J. and Nyssens, M. (2017). "Fundamentals for an International Typology of Social Enterprise Models", *VOLUNTAS: International Journal of Voluntary and Nonprofit Organizations*, 28 (6), 2469–2497. https://doi.org/10.1007/s11266-017-9884-7

Déneulin, S. (2014). *Well-Being, Justice and Development Ethics*, London: Routledge.

Déneulin, S. and McGregor, J. A. (2010). "The Capability Approach and the Politics of a Social Conception of Wellbeing", *European Journal of Social Theory*, 13 (4), 501–519. https://doi.org/10.1177/1368431010382762

Erasmo, V. (2019). "The Foundational Decade to Amartya Sen's Capability Approach (1970–1980)", *Rivista di Storia Economica*, 35 (3), 295–326. https://doi.org/10.1410/98221

Erasmo, V. (2021). "Mutual Recognition: the missing link from the "is" of capabilities to the "ought" of rights. An analysis of Amartya Sen and Paul Ricoeur's "dialogue"", *Critical Hermeneutics*, 5 (2), 247–276. https://doi.org/10.13125/ch/4673

Erasmo, V. (2022). "Amartya Sen's Earlier Conception of Economic Agents Through the Origins and Development of His Capability Approach (1970–1993)", *Erasmus Journal for Philosophy and Economics*, 15 (1), 184–193.

Erasmo, V. (2023). "My Well-being is (Not) as Important as Yours": Self-sacrifice as Further Economic Motive in Amartya Sen's Thought". In *Research in the History of Economic Thought and Methodology: Including a Selection of Papers Presented at the First History of Economics Diversity Caucus Conference*, Emerald Publishing Limited. https://doi.org/10.1108/S0743-41542023000041B004

Erasmo, V. (2024). "'Who Are the Capability Theorists?': A Tale of the Origins and Development of the Capability Approach", *Cambridge Journal of Economics*, 48 (3), 425–450. https://doi.org/10.1093/cje/beae004

Erasmo, V. (2025). "Extending the Capabilities Conception of the Individual in Economics: Relationality and Responsibility", *Journal of Interdisciplinary Economics*, 37 (1), 25–41. https://doi.org/10.1177/02601079231179372

Erasmo, V. (2026). "From Fact/Value Entanglement to the Revival of Classical Political Economy: Walsh's Contribution to the Capability Approach Literature", *Cambridge Journal of Economics*. 50 (4), 763–786. https://doi.org/10.1093/cje/beag019

Erasmo, V. and Migheli, M. (2026). "Reading Social Enterprises (SEs) Through Sen's Notion of Commitment", *Journal of Economic Interaction and Coordination*, 1–20.

Erasmo, V. and Santori, P. (2025). "What Should a Liberal Economist (Not) Do? Sen–Sugden Debate on Welfare Economics", *Cambridge Journal of Economics*, 49 (4), 849–872. https://doi.org/10.1093/cje/beaf023

Folbre, N. (1994). *Who Pays for the Kids? Gender and the Structures of Constraint*, London: Routledge.

Gasper, D. (2020). "*Amartya Sen, Social Theorizing and Contemporary India*", International Institute of Social Sciences, Working Paper, n. 658.

Granovetter, M. (1985). "Economic Action and Social Structure: The Problem of Embeddedness", *American Journal of Sociology*, 91 (3), 481–510.

Hédoin, C. (2016). "Sen's Criticism of Revealed Preference Theory and Its 'Neo-Samuelsonian Critique': A Methodological and Theoretical Assessment", *Journal of Economic Methodology*, 23 (4), 349–373. https://doi.org/10.1080/1350178X.2016.1218530

Kneafsey, M., Venn, L., Schmutz, U., Balázs, B., Trenchard, L., Eyden-Wood, T., … and Blackett, M. (2013). "Short Food Supply Chains and Local Food Systems in the EU. A State of Play of Their Socio-Economic Characteristics", *JRC Scientific and Policy Reports*, 123, 129.

Kuklys, W. (2004). "Measuring Standard of Living in the UK-An Application of Sen's Functioning Approach Using Structural Equation Models (No. 2004-11)". Max Planck Institute of Economics, Strategic Interaction Group. Measuring Standard of Living in the UK - An Application of Sen's Functioning Approach Using Structural Equation Models.

Kuklys, W. (2005). *Amartya Sen's Capability Approach: Theoretical Insights and Empirical Applications*, Berlin: Springer.
Laville, J. L. (2010). "The Solidarity Economy: An International Movement", *RCCS Annual Review. A Selection from the Portuguese Journal Revista Crítica de Ciências Sociais*, 2. https://doi.org/10.4000/rccsar.202
Nussbaum, M. (1992). "Human Functioning and Social Justice: in Defense of Aristotelian Essentialism", *Political Theory*, 20 (2), 202–246. https://doi.org/10.1177/0090591792020002002
Nussbaum, M. (1999). "Women and Equality: the Capabilities Approach", *International Labor Review*, 138 (3), 45–65.
Nussbaum, M. (2003). "Capabilities as Fundamental Entitlements: Sen and Social Justice", *Feminist Economics*, 9 (2–3), 33–59.
Pressman, S. and Summerfield, G. (2002). "Sen and Capabilities", *Review of Political Economy*, 14 (4), 429–434. https://doi.org/10.1080/09538250220000009889
Putnam, H. (2002). *The Collapse of the Fact/Value Dichotomy and Other Essays*, Harvard: Harvard University Press.
Qizilbash, M. (2007). "Social Choice and Individual Capabilities", *Politics, Philosophy & Economics*, 6 (2), 169–192. https://doi.org/10.1177/1470594X07077271
Rawls, J. (1971). *A Theory of Justice: Revised Edition*, Harvard: Harvard University Press (1999). https://doi.org/10.2307/j.ctvkjb25m
Robeyns, I. (2003). "Sen's Capability Approach and Gender Inequality: Selecting Relevant Capabilities", *Feminist Economics*, 9 (2–3), 61–92.
Robeyns, I. (2017). *Well-Being, Freedom and Social Justice: The Capability Approach Re-Rexamined*, Open-book Publishers.
Robeyns, I. and Brighouse, H. (2010) "Introduction: Social Primary Goods and Capabilities as Metrics of Justice". In Robeyns, I. and Brighouse, H. (eds.), *Measuring Justice: Primary Goods and Capabilities*, Cambridge: Cambridge University Press, pp. 1–13.
Robeyns, I. and Byskov, M. F. (2020). "The Capability Approach". In *Stanford Encyclopaedia of Philosophy*. Accessed on February 23, 2026. The Capability Approach (Stanford Encyclopedia of Philosophy).
Saigaran, N. G., Karupiah, P. and Gopal, P. S. (2015). "The Capability Approach: Comparing Amartya Sen and Martha Nussbaum", *Proceedings of Universiti Sains Malaysia*, 1–8.
Sen, A. (1980). *Equality of What?, Tanner Lecture on Human Values*, vol. 1, Cambridge University Press, 195–220.
Sen, A. (1985a). *Commodities and Capabilities*, Amsterdam: North Holland.
Sen, A. (1985b). "The Moral Standing of the Market". In *Ethics and Economics*, Oxford: Basil Blackwell, pp. 1–19.
Sen, A. (1993). *Inequality Re-examined*, Cambridge: Cambridge University Press.
Sen, A. and Dasgupta, S. (1983). "Malnutrition of Rural Children and the Sex Bias", *Economic and Political Weekly*, 18 (19–21), 855–864.
Senyard, J., Baker, T., Steffens, P. and Davidsson, P. (2014). "Bricolage as a Path to Innovativeness for Resource-Constrained New Firms", *Journal of Product Innovation Management*, 31 (2), 211–230. https://doi.org/10.1111/jpim.12091
Shapiro, I. (2011). "Review of The Idea of Justice, by Amartya Sen", *Journal of Economic Literature*, 49 (4), 1251–1263. https://www.jstor.org/stable/23071672
Sintomer, Y., Herzberg, C., Röcke, A. and Allegretti, G. (2012). "Transnational Models of Citizen Participation: The Case of Participatory Budgeting", *Journal of Deliberative Democracy*, 8 (2). https://doi.org/10.16997/jdd.141

Sugden, R. (1993). "Welfare, Resources and Capabilities: A Review of 'Inequality Re-examined' by Amartya Sen", *Journal of Economic Literature*, 31, 1947–1962.

Walsh, V. (1961). *Scarcity and Evil*, Englewood Cliffs: Prentice Hall.

Wampler, B. (2012). "Participation, Representation, and Social Justice: Using Participatory Governance to Transform Representative Democracy", *Polity*, 44 (4), 666–682. https://doi.org/10.1057/pol.2012.21

Zamagni, S. (2021). "The Quest for an Axiological Reorientation of Economic Science", *Structural Change and Economic Dynamics*, 58, 391–401. https://doi.org/10.1016/j.strueco.2021.06.011

1 Economic agents and economic motives from ancient philosophy to contemporary economics

1.1 Introduction

The analysis of economic motives has always been a complex issue in economics. At the core of this analysis lies the assumption that economic behavior is not deterministic (Dickinson, 1922). When there is the freedom to choose how to behave, there is also the possibility to properly talk about "the role of economic motives in decision-making". This chapter will provide a brief historical overview of the main analyses around economic motives, from Ancient philosophy to contemporary economics, thereby providing the intellectual context within which Sen's contribution can be situated.

This chapter is composed as follows: Section 1.2 offers a historical description of the origins and evolution of the early analysis of economic behavior in Ancient Greek philosophy, from Aristotle to the Pelagians. Subsequently, Section 1.3 shows how Aristotle influenced Thomas Aquinas and Antonio Genovesi, who extended the Aristotelian analysis of economic motives and agents in the context of the civil economy tradition. Section 1.4, instead, focuses on Adam Smith and the early formulations of *homo oeconomicus*.

This historical overview provides the necessary background for introducing Sen's notion of commitment (in Chapter 2), which forms the theoretical basis for his understanding of (embedded) economic agents.

Which economic motives are usually considered in economics? How are these economic motives related to understanding the economic agents adopted by a particular school of thought? These are some of the questions that this chapter will address. The story of philosophers and early economic thinkers who discussed economic motives and behavior is certainly broader than what can be covered here.[1] For this reason, we focus on those topics and figures that offer (or may offer) the most relevant contributions to introduce the discussion around Sen's notion of commitment and his embedded impartial spectator.

DOI: 10.4324/9781003381099-2

1.2 The origins of economic motives in Ancient economic thought: from Aristotle to the Pelagians

The historical origins of the theoretical analysis of economic motives are rooted in Ancient philosophy. In particular, Aristotle was the first to systematically study human behavior in economics (Van Staveren, 2013). After Aristotle, however, other thinkers had continued to engage with economic issues, particularly the concept of human needs (Rowe, 2005). Understanding the origins and satisfaction of these needs was considered crucial for explaining economic motives and behavior in Ancient economic thought. For instance, the Pelagians regarded the concept of needs, the basis of contemporary economic discipline, as a means to better specify human nature. For them, needs also had an anthropological dimension. In particular, "human needs are negative capabilities requiring responsive social conditions and, therefore, in most instances, social changes for their fulfillment" (Springborg, 1984, p. 394). However, we should proceed gradually.

In *Politics,* instead, Aristotle described human needs as the set of motivations (including the economic ones) and the direction of human life that swing between spontaneous and ungoverned aspirations and desires that might lead to conflict in a community of scarce resources. Thus, satisfying human needs is essential for safeguarding harmony in a society (Christie, 1997). The context where these motivations arise is the specific social system where an individual is "embedded", bound to the historical structures devoted to producing and distributing goods and services. For this reason, human needs are intrinsically economic because they are related to scarce resources. So, the idea of embeddedness in economics had already implicitly arisen in Ancient philosophy.

Aristotle stressed that needs are fundamentally heterogeneous. Governments often fail when attempting to address them. The struggle to reconcile these needs persists even in the Modern Age, with scholars like Hegel and the contractarians. Thus, Aristotle argued that State's intervention to satisfy human needs is essential for maintaining social harmony. According to his political theory, the satisfaction of human needs contributes to the flourishing of human nature. However, this process "cannot be realized outside of the State" (Everson, 1988, p. 89). For Aristotle, the satisfaction of human needs is more than an economic issue; it is also a problem of justice because, without satisfying these needs, it is impossible to live a good life.

The theoretical system where Aristotle discussed human needs also includes wants and desires that refer to everyday life, which we will call, alongside the civil economy tradition, a 'civil society' where individuals follow their goals and interests (Edwards, 2009). So, the analysis of human needs assumed an ethical, political, and social dimension in Ancient philosophy because they are one of the leading causes for human association in the dynamics of mutual exchanges of economic and social goods which are often tacit. In particular, basic needs are always analysed in terms of their fulfilment, but they are oriented to promote human flourishing and excellence for all the members of society (Rowe, 2005). But we must proceed gradually, distinguishing the nature of basic needs and how they are satisfied in economics from achieving human flourishing in society.

For Aristotle, having basic needs is natural, and fulfilling them implies a modest income (Skidelsky and Skidelsky, 2012), without leading to a leisurely existence. In this context, those who helped society satisfy their basic needs as slaves were not leading a humbling job; rather, it was a virtuous activity (Reader, 2005). The first place where human needs are satisfied is family,[2] as Aristotle wrote in the *Politics*

> The family is the association established by nature for the supply of men's everyday needs. [...] When several families are united, and the association aims at something more than the supply of daily needs, the first society to be formed is the village. [...] When several villages are united in a single complete, community, large enough to be nearly or quite self-sufficient, the state comes into existence, originating in the bare needs of life, and continuing in existence for the sake of a good life.
>
> (1252bl3-30)

We should contextualize this idea of satisfying human needs within Aristotle's broader view of what "economic/s" and "economy" mean. Aristotle was one of the first thinkers in Western philosophy to focus on "economic" rather than the "economy". In particular, Aristotle coined the Greek term *oikonomiké*, which is not substantive enough to convey what we define through the English term "economy". Instead, it is an adjective that might be translated as the English adjective "economic", as Bruni, Zamagni, and Santori stress (2021). In this respect, Aristotle introduced the notion of *oikonomia* in the first book of *Politics*. He referred to *oikos*, namely the household understood as a good, and as those interpersonal relationships that *are established* within it, for instance, such as those of wife–husband, father–sons, and boss–slaves (Aristotle, 2001). These relationships were established in the same space where other economic phenomena occurred, namely the *polis*. In other words, the city is where human flourishing, which includes the satisfaction of human needs, is realized, leading people to a condition of *eudaimonia* (happiness), the highest good for Aristotle. According to this Aristotelian understanding of happiness in terms of human flourishing, *eudaimonia* also becomes synonymous with living a "good life" (Scott, 2013), a life well lived where human existence is considered as a whole, not as an emotion or a psychological (transitory) condition (Sachs, 2021). This element represents a first step towards what we define today as happiness economics (Graham, 2005). In other words, individuals are *zoon politikon* (or political animals) and interpersonal relationships, with family, friends, and other citizens, are necessary for happiness (Bruni, 2008).

However, Aristotle stressed that these relationships should be based on the moral virtue of justice for leading individuals to happiness. It is impossible to fulfil a good life without justice (Winthrop, 1978). In Aristotle, the moral virtue of justice is a complex and articulated notion. For the sake of simplicity, we will only focus on his general understanding of justice, for which:

> justice (…) is complete excellence, only not without qualification but in relation to another person. It is because of this that justice is often thought to be the mightiest of the excellences, so that "neither Evening Star nor Morning equals its wonder," and as the proverb says: "In justice is every virtue gathered."
>
> (Aristotle, *Nicomachean Ethics* reproduced in Schofield, p. 313)

The concept of justice in social relationships will also be at the cornerstone of civil economy, which we will better explore in Section 1.3, but also in Chapter 6. The excellence of justice refers to the excellence of interpersonal relationships that align with the Aristotelian idea of individuals as political animals, for whom happiness depends on the main social relationships established with others (family, friends, and citizens). Individuals cannot live a good life without this excellence of social relationships grounded in justice. Aristotle argued in *Politics* that a happy life is lived together with others. Someone might possess every good, but without friendship, there is no real space for happiness (Sachs, 2021).

In the realization of a virtuous life, pleasure is not rejected because a virtuous life is a source of pleasure in itself (Cruz Ortiz de Landázuri, 2014). However, pleasure is moderated under the guidance of another virtue, temperance (*sophrosyne*) (Bloomfield, 2024). In this Aristotelian view of social relationships and their role in achieving happiness, we should not neglect the role of practical wisdom (*phronesis*) because individuals are always responsible for choosing the right actions towards *eudaimonia* (Nagel, 1972). For this reason, *phronesis* also has important implications for economic behavior, as it orients individuals towards ethical or unethical behavior, and this is the basis of every choice, including the economic ones (Noel, 1999).

Aristotle's contribution to early economic thinking is not limited to the analysis of issues, such as human needs and social relationships; he also interestingly explores how economics interacts with other social sciences. In this regard, Aristotle suggested that economics should be cooperative mainly with practical disciplines aimed at human good acting, as the handmaid of politics, which seems to be subject to the most comprehensive framework, so its goal will include that of other sciences, such as the human good (Aristotle, 2009).

As anticipated, Aristotle was not in favour of a leisurely life. For this reason, economics does not have the ultimate aim to fulfil wealth only, as in modern economics. In *Politics,* Aristotle argued that "when money becomes an intermediary element in exchange, the natural limits on physical wants cease to exercise restraint on desires, and the unlimited desire for wealth results in a lack of natural restraint" (Lowry, 1979, p. 68). However, this unlimited desire for wealth should be limited to avoid vicious, individualistic behavior that would also be self-interested and antisocial. According to Aristotle, economics should instead cooperate with other arts to realize a more important goal: the so-called "common end", namely the common good, making it possible to promote the flourishing of human existence for more people. This flourishing is understood in terms of *eudaimonia*, chosen by individuals for the sake of happiness itself and not for the benefit of others, as happiness is complete (Farwell, 1995). In particular, economics has what we might define today as a "co-partnership" with politics in pursuit of the common good (Raskin, 2019). At the same time, economics originates in ethics, particularly in the ethical understanding of politics (Sen, 1987). The economic issues we can identify in Aristotle are broader than those analysed in this chapter, including concepts such as use and exchange values (Miller, 1998). This discussion suffices to conclude our analysis of Aristotle here, emphasizing that the dialogue between economics and other social sciences was already relevant in Ancient philosophy, including in the study of economic motives.

1.3 The analysis of economic motives and behavior from Thomas Aquinas to the modern civil economy tradition

During the Middle Ages, Aristotle exercised a decisive influence on economic thinking. The philosopher and theologian Thomas of Aquinas was most influenced by him (Neves, 2000). This figure deserves attention because he was among the forerunners of the modern civil economy tradition. Aquinas further developed the Aristotelian idea of economic agents as *zoon politikon* in the context of the so-called "Mediterranean spirit of capitalism" (Santori, 2021). In this respect, Aquinas rejected altruism and egoism as possible economic motives for economic behavior, developing an anthropological perspective where reciprocity is the cornerstone of civil life (Bruni, 2014). In particular, Aquinas suggested that reciprocity is a foundational virtue for mutual assistance in economics and politics, promoting the common good. So, reciprocity is realized, on the one hand, in economics through a mutual concern in market dynamics because "mutual assistance manifests in market exchanges along with self-interest" (Santori, 2021, p. 20); on the other hand, in politics, institutions become reciprocal with their citizens participating in the promotion of the common good (Erasmo, 2022).

Thus, self-interest exists as an economic motive, but it is softened thanks to dimensions like "gifts—gratuitousness, authenticity, trust, genuine sociality, intrinsic motivation—permeate the economic realm of contract based on self-interest" (Santori, 2021, p. 142). For this reason, this non-conflictual coexistence of gifts and contracts, particularly in economics, might be summarized through the formula of "gift and contracts intertwined" (Santori, 2021, p. 142). This co-existence of contracts and gifts enables reciprocity in terms of mutual assistance within markets and political life, giving rise to a civil understanding of the society where individuals and institutions are equally engaged in promoting the common good through a strong sense of responsibility for this purpose.

Some years later, in the late modern age, we witnessed the official birth of economics as a discipline, shifting from economic thought to economics (Bruni et al., 2021). The term "political economy" was initially coined by Antoine de Montchrestien (1575–1621). However, the economic discipline was historically institutionalized only with Antonio Genovesi, among the leading exponents of modern civil economy, who occupied the first European chair in Economics in 1754. This "institutionalization" of economics distinguishes this discipline from philosophy and other social sciences, thanks to a progressive and constant process of formalizing its concepts and theories (Mirowski, 1991).

The institutionalization of economic discipline affected the discussions on economic motives. With Genovesi, the analysis of economic motives developed more significantly than in the Middle Ages because he explicitly elaborated a new understanding of economic agents within the civil economy framework, defining individuals in terms of *homo reciprocans*. Not unlike Aquinas, Genovesi (1769 [2013], *Lezioni di commercio o sia di economia civile*) argued that the market was a space for mutuality; in turn, reciprocity could be found in the dynamics of mutual assistance among members of the same community. The originality of Genovesi, compared to the early civil economy tradition, lies in his explicit reference to economic agents as *homo reciprocans* in the light of those social relationships that individuals establish in their community based on reciprocity (Fehr and Gächter, 1998).

We do not find a new systematic anthropological paradigm for describing economic agents in the discussed so far thinkers. This absence may be explained by the need to offer an alternative to the Hobbesian assumption of *homo homini lupus* (man as an enemy of other men) elaborated during the Modern Age (Höffe, 2015). Against the idea that individuals are self-interested and in conflict with one another in a kind of primitive "state of nature", Genovesi endorsed "natural sociability and the political nature of human society, including the political bodies that constitute the civil realm" (Pabst, 2018, p. 583).

Being a *homo reciprocans* means to be a social economic agent, and this intrinsic sociality also applies to the division of labor and other activities, for instance, such as trade and production. In this direction, Genovesi revisited Aristotle's view of the *polis* grounded in *philia* (friendship) and oriented towards human happiness to argue that the market is likewise built on friendship, and the aim is to promote public happiness (Crespo, 2014).

Public happiness became the core idea of the Italian Enlightenment, which mainly flourished between Naples and Milan, the most critical intellectual milieux of the modern civil economy tradition during the second half of the 18th century. Among the proponents of the market as the ideal place for promoting public happiness were the prominent Italian economists of those years: not only Antonio Genovesi but also Cesare Beccaria, Ferdinando Galiani, and Pietro Verri (Porta, 2016).

In this framework, institutions were equally committed to the goal of "common prosperity" and "public good" related to fulfilling mutual benefit. This fulfilment, in turn, is promoted by intrinsic social reciprocity, which ranges from reciprocal needs to reciprocal obligation to assist each other, which characterizes human nature (Nalli, 2023). What brings together the members of a particular society and institutions for promoting common prosperity and the public good is what Genovesi (1769 [2013]) defined as "public trust" (*fede pubblica*, which includes ethical, economic, and political trust) that makes it possible to appreciate civil life, but also the spirit of industry, for a condition of abundance for everybody.

Unlike Adam Smith (whom we will explore in Section 1.4), Genovesi believed that trade is mutually beneficial and becomes the foundation of the wealth of nations (Bruni and Sugden, 2000). In this respect, trust makes reciprocal reliability in trade possible, thereby increasing society's wealth. Conversely, without public trust, "society cannot nurture 'the taste for civil life, and thus the spirit of industry, which brings about the opulence of the State (il gusto del vivere civile, e quindi lo spirito industrial, che cagionano l'opulenza dello Stato)' (Genovesi, 2013, p. 342)" (Pabst, 2018, p. 584). Thus, public trust strengthens bonds among families and citizens towards the common good, as well as "common happiness" (*comune felicità*), grounded in individual responsibility towards the others, not just on institutions' power. However, individual responsibility is only partially inborn in human nature, which differs from the self-interested understanding of individuals elaborated by Hobbes. Rather, individual responsibility is also enhanced thanks to public education. This element explains why we cannot avoid a comparison with the civil economy tradition, where individual responsibility for promoting the common good appears to be even more substantial than the sense of responsibility of institutions themselves.

Before introducing Adam Smith and other modern economic thinkers who provided insights on economic motives and agents, it is important to emphasize that the *fil rouge* of the contemporary civil economy tradition lies primarily in the public dimension in social and economic life. Through this shift away from a private dimension of human existence, society as a whole became oriented towards promoting the common good/common happiness based on individuals' universal sympathy towards each other. Aquinas, and later the modern civil economy, introduced concepts we will not find in the classical and neoclassical economy, such as common good, mutual assistance, public happiness, public trust, reciprocity, and virtue, which are seminal for discussing an embedded understanding of economic agents.

1.4 The evolution of economic motives in modern political economy: focusing on Adam Smith and his impartial spectator

Between the XVIII and the XIX centuries, economics became an independent discipline, destined even to become the most mature social science in the contemporary age (Fuchs and Turner, 1986). However, economics as an independent discipline did not entirely neglect its constitutive ethical dimensions, including the analysis of economic motives and the consequences of economic behavior. For instance, Adam Smith, John Stuart Mill, Karl Marx, and Francis Ysidro Edgeworth also provided ethical answers compared to economic questions even as normative issues in economics progressively marginalized in economic analysis (Walsh, 2000).

Among these pivotal scholars, we focus on Adam Smith because he was one of those figures who influenced Amartya Sen and his understanding of economic motives and economic agents. Smith was a particularly controversial and fascinating philosopher and economist who explored economic motives and the nature of economic agents in the Modern Age. The key reference text for understanding these concepts is his *Theory of Moral Sentiments* (1759). In his masterpiece, Smith referred to economic agents by emphasizing their natural sympathy towards others. His optimistic understanding of economic agents was closer to the Aristotelian rather than the Hobbesian one. Sympathy is an economic motive with a broad meaning, from representing the basis of human nature to explaining the role of moral judgment (Montes, 2003). Given this breadth, the concept has sparked a lively dialogue in the literature: According to Raphael (1985), sympathy is the cement for society, but merely a criterion of moral approval or disapproval; in contrast, Khalil (1990) admits that sympathy is also a motivation for action. We share this second broader alternative in this book.

In particular, Smith's sympathy is a spontaneous process in which individuals

> exercise sympathy not only when foreseeing pleasure or any outcome as an end (to avoid a utilitarian or hedonistic connotation). The final cause of the sympathetic process is a *telos* understood in the Aristotelian sense, not as a simple attainment of an end, but as "contributing to it," for its own sake.
>
> (Montes, 2003, p. 83)

Thus, it would be incorrect to define Smith's sympathy in means-to-ends terms, since the sympathetic process is not limited to a concordance (or non-concordance) of sentiments between two individuals. This interpretation of sympathy explains why this concept cannot be reduced to moral approval or disapproval. However, this element does not invalidate the sympathetic process. Rather, were sympathy limited to the exercise of moral judgments, individuals would be deprived of the moral autonomy integral to Smith's ethical system, embodied by his concept of the 'impartial spectator'.

Thus, economic agents should be impartial in their moral judgments and economic decisions. Impartiality is undoubtedly pivotal in Adam Smith's analysis of moral sentiments (Evensky, 2005). In the following quotation, Smith adopted the term "impartial" for the first time in one of his masterpieces. This introduction characterizes a series of concepts directly related to the dimension of sight or that might be experienced through sight, such as 'eyes', 'look', 'observation', 'to view', 'candid', and 'light'. For this reason, we will explore what we might define as the 'impartial light of the spectator's sight' in this comment.

> As nature teaches the spectators to assume the circumstances of the person principally concerned, so she teaches this last in some measure to assume those of the spectators. (…) As their sympathy makes them look at it [his own situation], in some measure, with his eyes, so his sympathy makes him look at it, in some measure, with theirs, especially when in their presence, and acting under their observation: and as the reflected passion, which he thus conceives, is much weaker than the original one, it necessarily abates the violence of what he felt before he came into their presence, before he began to recollect in what manner they would be affected by it, and to view his situation in this candid and impartial light.
>
> (Smith, 1759, p. 29)

This quotation opens one of the few key passages in The Theory of Moral Sentiments (TMS) in which Smith used the plural noun to refer to the figure of the spectator (Raphael, 2007). Although there is still no explicit reference to sight and impartiality, Smith implicitly suggested the existence of a kind of two-sided eye where "nature teaches the spectator to assume the circumstances of the person principally concerned", such as the 'agent' or the 'actor'; but, at the same time, nature teaches the actor to assume "in some measure (…) those of the spectators" (Smith, 1759, p. 29). Within this dynamic, we may find a double visual movement: on the one hand, from the spectator to the actor; on the other hand, from the actor to the spectator. This two-sided eye derives from the harmony of feelings between actor and spectator through mutual sympathy (Mueller, 2016, p. 315). In Smith, mutual sympathy is the source of the spectator's moral judgment. It represents the foundation for our concerns for others, leading us to form an idea about "how others feel by considering how we would feel in like circumstances" (Coase, 1976, p. 529), since it is an act of imagination. This act puts us in others' place, although the feelings deriving from imagination will not certainly have the same intensity as theirs, but they will be weaker than the original one (Smith, 1759, p. 29).

In another passage of the TMS, Smith argued that this act of imagination derives right from the experience of viewing ourselves through the "eyes of other people, or as other people are likely to view" (Smith, 1759, p. 133). Thus, the sympathetic process might be reasonably understood as a two-sided eye through which we look at others and vice versa to imagine others' feelings. However, the mentioned above quotation tells us something more about the sympathetic process because it makes, on the one hand, the spectators "*look*" at the actor's situation "in some measure, with his *eyes*" (Smith, 1759, p. 29); on the other hand, at the same time, the actor "*look*[*s*]" at his situation "with theirs, especially when in their presence, and acting under their *observation*" (Smith, 1759, p. 29). The sympathetic process is, therefore, characterized by an asymmetric sight because this two-sided eye between the actor and the spectator makes them respectively look only "in some measure" with others' eyes.

Interestingly, this asymmetry reduces when the actor acts under the spectators' observation. The physical presence of the spectators makes the actor get closer to their sight about his situation. However, being closer to others enables the actor to *see* himself from a certain distance (Hanley, 2019). In this way, it is like the actor stepping outside himself to gain the same perspective the others have on his life. This perspective offers the appropriate (or correct) distance to observe his situation because "being too close or too far away from a situation does not adequately constrain the violence of our passions" (Paganelli, 2010).

Too little distance leads to laxness and partiality in judgments, while excessive distance leads to judgment biases. Instead, the eyes of others upon the actor make him view his situation from an appropriate distance in a "candid and impartial light" (Smith, 1759, p. 29). Thanks to the others' observation, the actor can finally look impartially at his situation (Gerschlager, 2005) because the reflected passion becomes much weaker than the original one, and he sees his situation clearly. However, observing others in their presence allows the actor to observe his situation from an appropriate distance in a "candid and impartial light" where the reflected passions are weaker and his judgments become, in turn, impartial.

According to Smith (1759), sympathy and the impartial spectator have a social dimension because they connect individuals to society. In particular, morality is linked to cognitive and social processes, in which others' approval is pivotal. Thus, individual behaviors are based on the perceptions of others, and actions are simultaneously adjusted to obtain their sympathy (Rathbone, 2018). Smith referred to this cognitive process when he proposed that the impartial spectator formulates moral judgments. Accordingly, Smith's impartial spectator is a spontaneous sympathetic subject whose corresponding process is neither a merciful action nor a kind of benevolence. Instead, this is an example of closeness to others' feelings, thoughts, and experiences. Moral judgment, in turn, is socially embodied in the moral codes that arise through social interactions which may also modify individual motivations. Hence, we affirm that Smith's morality depends on social experiences that, in turn, are essential for a civil economy perspective on individuals in economics.

Between the XVIII and the XIX centuries, other representations of economic agents arose, characterized by a less optimistic and less cooperative understanding of the individuals. Philosophers and economists like Jeremy Bentham, David Hume, Carl Menger, John Stuart Mill, Vilfredo Pareto, and Léon Walras contributed to the elaboration of *homo oeconomicus*. Pareto likely coined this term for the first time (Bee and Desmarais-Tremblay, 2023). In this respect, Benthamite hedonistic psychology foreshadowed this paradigm, where individuals mainly maximize their pleasure (Baujard, 2014). According to this view, economic agents are focused on acquiring and consuming material goods, while their primary goal is to improve individual wealth, instead of collective well-being as in the abovementioned perspectives based on Aristotelian values. This understanding of economic agents perfectly fits with neoclassical theories leading to social atomism.

From a methodological profile, *homo oeconomicus* became a successful representation of economic agents alongside the consolidation of the engineeristic approach in economics, fostered by the rise of physics as a scientific discipline (Mariotti, 2021). Based on this consolidation, the analysis of normative issues became marginalized in economics, influencing, in turn, the very same idea about the nature of economic agents. Individuals are no longer understood as social, responsible, and reciprocal in their economic decisions towards promoting the common good/happiness. Concepts related to the social dimension disappeared from the economic jargon in favour of rational behavior based on a self-interested maximization of individual utility.

Alongside this methodological explanation for the rise of *homo oeconomicus* within the flourishing of the engineeristic approach in economics, additional reasons help explain the success of this paradigm. On the one hand, there was the triumph of the avalutativity of morality within Anglo-Saxon liberalism; on the other hand, conversely, *homo oeconomicus* became the representative understanding of economic agents for marginalist economists, where self-interest became the prominent economic motive in individual decision-making (Giovanola, 2013). The advent of *homo oeconomicus* led to significant changes in the understanding of economic motives and economic agents. For instance, social interactions were no longer central as in the tradition from Aristotle to the civil economy tradition, since individualism replaced reciprocity in economic decisions to maximize individual utility through self-interested behavior. In a certain sense, *homo oeconomicus* makes economic agents, once again, under the logic of the Hobbesian "homo homini lupus". However, this understanding of economic agents should be located not in a pessimistic anthropology of human nature but rather in a different sense of "rationality" in economics.

Elster (1979) offered an interesting reading of individual rationality, associating *homo oeconomicus* with the mythological figure of Ulysses and the episode of the Sirens. Ulysses was conflicted between the desire to hear the Sirens' song and the awareness of the consequences of this action. According to neoclassical rationality, Ulysses adopted a rational choice strategy following Circe's recommendation. In this episode, Ulysses agrees to tie himself to the pole and orders his men not to listen to the Sirens' song. In other words, Ulysses realizes a rational calculation for finding the most suitable tools for achieving his goals. At the same time, this choice temporarily deprived Ulysses of his freedom to move, while his men suffered huge inequalities because Ulysses was the only one who might be delighted by the Sirens' beautiful song. This mythological figure is an example of strict economic rationality that characterizes mainstream *homo oeconomicus* (Elster, 1979), who prefers individual and self-interested behavior in a condition of informative completeness. However, this represents a reductionist perspective on economic agents, where rationality is mainly instrumental rather than ethical, as in Aristotle's early formulation of *phronesis*.

1.5 Concluding remarks

As has emerged in this chapter, the philosopher who contributed most to the development of some preliminary ideas about economic issues during the Ancient age is undoubtedly Aristotle, discussing in-depth concepts like human needs, economy/economics, social relationships, happiness, justice, practical wisdom, and so on. All these elements show how Aristotle already conceptualized economic behavior within Greek philosophical thought. In particular, he assigned a privileged role to social relationships that contribute to individuals' human flourishing. In turn, social relationships are seminal for satisfying human needs that directly orient individuals' choices, including the economic ones. Thus, relationality not only makes individuals happy but also helps satisfy their economic needs. Subsequently, Aristotle exerted a strong influence on Thomas Aquinas, in whose thought concepts such as mutuality emerged. These same concepts would later re-emerge in the modern tradition of civil economy.

All these authors shared a common focus on social relationships as means of improving the individuals' quality of life and contributing to the promotion of collective wealth, thereby strengthening the markets. However, the advent of *homo oeconomicus* replaced this optimistic view of human nature, a self-interested individual oriented to the maximization of individual utility. Today, such formulations of *homo oeconomicus* are no longer effective, because this is "an inaccurate, but potentially misleading, model of an economic agent because it disproportionately emphasizes the role of self-interest as a mechanism in individual and social choice" (Erasmo et al., 2023, p. 173). This anthropological reductionism (Becchetti and Cermelli, 2018) is grounded in an instrumental rationality that does not deal "with our normativity and emotionality, both of which are intentional, that is, they are about relations with our environment—natural, practical and social" (Archer, 2000, p. 4).

Amartya Sen's alternative understanding of economic agents represented a valuable challenge to the prevailing reductionism in economics during the 1980s. Through his notion of commitment as a central economic motive, Sen was among the first to shift the focus from self-interest to other non-self-interested economic motives in decision-making. However, we will explore more fully in Chapter 2.

Notes

1 To better explore these issues, among others, see Foley (2004), Herfeld (2026), and Hollis and Nell (2007).

2 However, it is only with modern rationalism – mainly through the advent of Enlightenment – that needs explicitly became a philosophical category that was at the cornerstone of the discussion around justice also in terms of human needs that should be satisfied (Pinker, 2018). We will come back to the analysis of human needs in modern philosophy in Section 1.3.

References

Archer, M. S. (2000). *Being Human: The Problem of Agency*. Cambridge: Cambridge University Press.

Aristotle. (2001). *Politics*, Roma: L'Erma di Bretschneider.

Aristotle. (2009). *The Nicomachean Ethics*, New York: Oxford University Press.

Baujard, A. (2014). "Collective Interest Versus Individual Interest in Bentham's Felicific Calculus. Questioning Welfarism and Fairness". In Faccarello, G. and Sturn, R. (eds.), *Studies in the History of Public Economics*, London: Routledge, pp. 71–98. https://doi.org/10.4324/9781315872216.

Becchetti, L. and Cermelli, M. (2018). "Civil Economy: Definition and Strategies for Sustainable Well-Living", *International Review of Economics*, 65 (3), 329–357. https://doi.org/10.1007/s12232-018-0299-6

Bee, M. and Desmarais-Tremblay, M. (2023). "The Birth of Homo oeconomicus: The Methodological Debate on the Economic Agent from JS Mill to V. Pareto", *Journal of the History of Economic Thought*, 45 (1), 1–26. https://doi.org/10.1017/S1053837221000535

Bloomfield, P. (2024), "Temperance, Continence, Weakness, Indulgence, Compulsion". In Timmons, M. (ed.), *Oxford Studies in Normative Ethics*, Clarendon: Oxford University Press, pp. 49–68.

Bruni, L. (2008). "Back to Happiness? Happiness, Eudaimonia, and Relational Goods". In Bruni L., Comim F. and Pugno M. (eds.), *Capabilities and Happiness*, Oxford: Oxford University Press, pp. 114–139.

Bruni, L. (2014). "The Value of Sociality: Economics and Relationality in the Light of the Economy of Communion", *Revista Portuguesa de Filosofia*, 70(1), 61–79. https://www.jstor.org/stable/23785810

Bruni, L., Santori, P. and Zamagni, S. (2021). *Lezioni di storia del pensiero economico un percorso dall'antichità al Novecento*, Roma: Città Nuova.

Bruni, L. and Sugden, R. (2000). "Moral Canals: Trust and Social Capital in the Work of Hume, Smith and Genovesi", *Economics and Philosophy*, 16 (1), 21–45. https://doi.org/10.1017/S0266267100000122

Christie, D. J. (1997). "Reducing Direct and Structural Violence: The Human Needs Theory", *Peace and Conflict: Journal of Peace Psychology*, 3 (4), 315–332. https://doi.org/10.1207/s15327949pac0304_1

Coase, R. H. (1976). "Adam Smith's View of Man", *Journal of Law and Economics*, 19 (3), 529–546. https://doi.org/10.1086/466886

Crespo, R. F. (2014). "The Genesis and the Ethos of the Market by L. Bruni", *History of Economics Review*, 60, 93–96.

Cruz Ortiz de Landázuri, M. M. (2014). "Virtue Without Pleasure? Aristotle and the Joy of a Noble Life", *Acta Philosophica: Rivista Internazionale di Filosofia*, 23 (1), 89–100.

Dickinson, Z. C. (1922). *Economic Motives: a Study in the Psychological Foundations of Economic Theory*, Harvard: Harvard University Press.

Edwards, M. (2009). *Civil Society*, Malden: Polity.

Elster, J. (1979). *Ulysses and the Sirens: Studies in Rationality and Irrationality*. Cambridge: Cambridge University Press.

Erasmo, V. (2022). "Paolo Santori, Thomas Aquinas and the Civil Economy Tradition: The Mediterranean Spirit of Capitalism (London: Routledge, 2021), pp. 174, $128 (hardcover). ISBN: 9780367376109", *Journal of the History of Economic Thought*, 44 (4), 667–670. https://doi.org/10.1017/S1053837222000207

Erasmo, V., Jordet, M. and Wdowin, J. (2023). "Where Are "We" in the Economy? Some Reflections on the Place of Moral Sentiments and the Commons in Redefining Economics". In Santori, P. and Rotondi, V. (eds.), *Rethinking Economics Starting from the Commons: Towards an Economics of Francesco*, Cham: Springer International Publishing, pp. 171–184.

Evensky, J. (2005). "Adam Smith's Theory of Moral Sentiments: On Morals and Why They Matter to a Liberal Society of Free People and Free Markets", *Journal of Economic Perspective*, 19 (3), 109–130.

Everson, S. (1988). "Aristotle on the Foundations of the State", *Political Studies*, 36 (1), 89–101.

Farwell, P. (1995). "Aristotle and the Complete Life", *History of Philosophy Quarterly*, 12 (3), 247–263, http://www.jstor.org/stable/27744665

Fehr, E. and Gächter, S. (1998). "Reciprocity and Economics: The Economic Implications of Homo Reciprocans", *European Economic Review*, 42 (3–5), 845–859.

Foley, D. (2004). "The Strange History of the Economic Agent", *The New School Economic Review*, 1 (1), 82–94.

Fuchs, S. and Turner, J. H. (1986). "What Makes a Science 'Mature'?: Patterns of Organizational Control in Scientific Production", *Sociological Theory*, 4 (2), 143–150.

Genovesi, A. (1769 [2013]), *Lezioni di commercio o sia di economia civile*, Milan: Vita e Pensiero.

Gerschlager, C. (2005). "Beyond Economic Man: Adam Smith's Concept of the Agent and the Role of Deception", *Cahiers d'économie politique*, 49 (2), 31–49.

Giovanola, B. (2013). *Oltre l'homo oeconomicus, lineamenti di etica economica*, Salerno: Orthotes.

Graham, C. (2005). "The Economics of Happiness Insights on Globalization from a Novel Approach", *World Economics*, 6 (3), 41–55.

Hanley, R. P. (2019). *Our Great Purpose: Adam Smith on Living a Better Life*, Princeton: Princeton University Press.

Herfeld, C. (2026). *Conversations on Rational Choice*, Cambridge: Cambridge University Press.

Höffe, O. (2015). *Thomas Hobbes*, New York: Suny Press.

Hollis, M. and Nell, E. (2007). *Rational Economic Man. A Philosophical Critique of Neo-Classical Economics*, Cambridge: Cambridge University Press.

Khalil, E. L. (1990). "Beyond Self-Interest and Altruism: A Reconstruction of Adam Smith's Theory of Human Conduct", *Economics & Philosophy*, 6 (2), 255–273. https://doi.org/10.1017/S0266267100001243

Lowry, S. T. (1979). "Recent Literature on Ancient Greek Economic Thought", *Journal of Economic Literature*, 17 (1), 65–86. https://www.jstor.org/stable/2723641

Mariotti, S. (2021). "Forging a New Alliance between Economics and Engineering", *Journal of Industrial and Business Economics*, 48 (4), 551–572. https://doi.org/10.1007/s40812-021-00187-w

Miller, F. D. (1998). "Was Aristotle the First Economist?, *Apeiron*, 31 (4), 387–398. https://doi.org/10.1515/APEIRON.1998.31.4.387

Mirowski, P. (1991). *More Heat Than Light: Economics as Social Physics, Physics as Nature's Economics*, Cambridge: Cambridge University Press.

Montes, L. (2003). *Adam Smith in Context: A Critical Reassessment of Some Central Components of His Thought*, New York: Palgrave Macmillan.

Mueller, P. D. (2016). "Adam Smith's Impartial Spectator", *Econ Journal Watch*, 13 (2), 312–318.

Nagel, T. (1972). "Aristotle on Eudaimonia", *Phronesis*, 17 (3), 252–259. https://www.jstor.org/stable/4181892

Nalli, F. (2023). "What Mutual Assistance Is, and What It Could Be in the Contemporary World", *Journal of Business Ethics*, 182 (4), 1041–1053. https://doi.org/10.1007/s10551-021-04936-8

Neves, J. L. C. (2000). "Aquinas and Aristotle's Distinction on Wealth", *History of Political Economy*, 32 (3), 649–657. https://muse.jhu.edu/article/13236.

Noel, J. (1999). "On the Varieties of Phronesis", *Educational Philosophy and Theory*, 31 (3), 273–289. https://doi.org/10.1111/j.1469-5812.1999.tb00466.x

Pabst, A. (2018). "Political Economy of Virtue: Civil Economy, Happiness and Public Trust in the Thought of Antonio Genovesi", *European Journal of the History of Economic Thought*, 25 (4), 582–604. https://doi.org/10.1080/09672567.2018.1487462

Paganelli, M. P. (2010). "The Moralizing Role of Distance in Adam Smith: The Theory of Moral Sentiments as Possible Praise of Commerce", *History of Political Economy*, 42 (3), 425–441. https://doi.org/10.1215/00182702-2010-019

Pinker, S. (2018). Enlightenment Now: The Case for Reason, Science, Humanism, and Progress, London: Penguin UK.

Porta, P. L. (2016), "The Idea of Happiness in Italy". In Bruni, L. and Porta, P. L. (eds.), *Handbook of Research Methods and Applications in Happiness and Quality of Life*, Cheltenham: Edward Elgar, pp. 499–520. https://doi.org/10.4337/9781783471171.00029

Raphael D. (1985) *Adam Smith*. Oxford: Oxford University Press.
Raphael, D. D. (2007). *The Impartial Spectator. Adam Smith's Moral Philosophy*, New York: Oxford University Press.
Raskin, M. G. (2019). *The Common Good: Its Politics, Policies and Philosophy*, London and New York: Routledge.
Rathbone, M. (2018). "Adam Smith, the impartial spectator and embodiment: Towards an economics of accountability and dialogue". *Religions*, 9 (4), 118.
Reader, S. (2005). "Aristotle on Necessities and Needs", *Royal Institute of Philosophy Supplement*, 57, 113–135. https://doi.org/10.1017/S1358246100009176
Rowe, C. (2005). "Needs and Ethics in Ancient Philosophy", *Royal Institute of Philosophy Supplement*, 57, 99–112. https://doi.org/10.1017/S135824610505705X
Sachs, J. (2021), "Aristotle, Eudaimonia, Neuroscience and Economics". In Bruni, L., De Rosa, D. and Smerilli, A. (eds.), *A Modern Guide to the Economics of Happiness*, Cheltenham: Edward Elgar, pp. 29–45.
Santori, S. (2021). *Thomas Aquinas and the Civil Economy Tradition: The Mediterranean Spirit of Capitalism*, London: Routledge.
Scott, D. (2013), "Aristotle on the Good-Life". In Sheffield, F. and Warren, J. (eds.), *Routledge Companion to Ancient Philosophy*, London: Routledge.
Sen, A. (1987). *On Ethics and Economics*, Oxford: Basil Blackwell.
Skidelsky, E. and Skidelsky, R. (2012). *How Much Is Enough? Money and the Good Life*, London: Penguin Books UK.
Smith, A. (1759). *The Theory of Moral Sentiments*, London: Penguin Books UK.
Springborg, P. (1984). "Aristotle and the Problem of Needs", *History of Political Thought*, 5 (3), 393–424.
Van Staveren, I. (2013). *The Values of Economics. An Aristotelian Perspective*, London: Routledge.
Walsh, V. C. (2000). "Smith After Sen", *Review of Political Economy*, 12 (1), 5–25, https://doi.org/10.1080/095382500106795
Winthrop, D. (1978). "Aristotle and Theories of Justice", *The American Political Science Review*, 72 (4), 1201–1216.

2 Exploring Sen's notion of commitment

Towards the embedded impartial spectator

2.1 Introduction

After analysing the main discussions on economic agents and economic motives from ancient philosophy to contemporary economics, we can now introduce Sen's contribution to these debates through his notion of commitment. In his view, commitment is the ideal economic motive to be adopted in decision-making. For this reason, we argue that commitment constitutes the foundation of Sen's alternative understanding of economic agents, in contrast to mainstream *homo oeconomicus*, namely what we define here as the "embedded impartial spectator". To explore the theoretical foundation of Sen's concept of commitment, we must return to its historical roots. In this respect, we suggest that Sen's notion of commitment has been influenced by Smith's notion of sympathy and Harsanyi's imaginative empathy.

In this chapter, we introduce Sen's notion of commitment, discussing the scholars who most influenced him in developing this idea, namely Adam Smith and John C. Harsanyi. More specifically, in Section 2.2, we explore Sen's notion of commitment and his broader analysis of other economic motives (for instance, self-interest and sympathy), including their consequences for individual decision-making. In Section 2.3, we provide a historical review of the broad literature on Sen's notion of commitment. We then distinguish between the concepts of empathy and sympathy to highlight the possible respective influence of Smith's sympathy (in Section 2.4) and Harsanyi's imaginative empathy (in Section 2.6) on Sen's notions of commitment and impartiality, including an intermediate comparison between Smith and Harsanyi on these concepts (in Section 2.5) to show their analogies and differences.

This joint influence shows how, through the notion of commitment as the leading economic motive in decision-making, Sen elaborated an embedded conception of the individual as a possible alternative to the social atomism that characterized the early formulations of *homo oeconomicus* (Davis, 2003, 2009, 2024).

DOI: 10.4324/9781003381099-3

2.2 Sen's discussion of rational economic motives and their consequences on individual decision-making

Our historical starting point is that Sen elaborated on the premises for his alternative understanding of economic agents between the Seventies and the Eighties. It was a gradual process that began with his discussion of the rational economic motives adopted by economic agents. In this analysis, Sen (1977b, 1985) admitted three rational motives: self-interest, sympathy, and commitment. Firstly, we should distinguish between sympathy and commitment. Quoting Sen's words:

> If the knowledge of torture of others makes you sick, it is a case of sympathy; if it does not make you feel personally worse off, but you think it is wrong and you are ready to do something to stop it, it is a case of commitment.
>
> (Sen, 1977b, p. 326)

Sympathy has principally an egoistic and psychological value because it implies that "one is oneself pleased at others' pleasure and pained at others' pain, and the pursuit of one's own utility may thus be helped by sympathetic action" (Sen, 1977b, p. 326). In turn, "when a person's sense of well-being is psychologically dependent on someone else's welfare, it is a case of sympathy" (Sen, 1977b, p. 328). Considering those elements, Sen (1977b, 1985) claimed that sympathy is an intermediate motive between neoclassical self-interest and unselfish altruism: Indeed, this motive leads to a maximization of individual utility hidden behind apparently unselfish preferences with the aim of improving individual well-being.

It is a little bit harder to analyse Sen's concept of commitment (1977b, 1985) because it has both an ethical and a political value. At the same time, commitment is a form of recognition of the injustice underlying certain behaviors and a sense of duty to stop them. In particular, Sen defines commitment "in terms of a person choosing an act that he believes will yield a lower level of personal welfare to him than an alternative that is also available to him" (Sen, 1977b, p. 327). This independence from someone else's welfare implies that others are not considered "means" for improving individual welfare, like sympathy. This point is close to the Aristotelian tradition that started in Ancient philosophy and flourished in the civil economy tradition. In this way, Sen created a new space for social relationships in contemporary economics.

All economic motives, in turn, have consequences on individual decision-making. In particular, Sen (1985) supported the idea that economic motives influence "three different kinds of 'privateness' for an agent's preference ordering" (Hédoin, 2016, p. 6), namely *self-centered welfare*, *self-welfare goal*, and *self-goal choice*. These concepts are defined by Sen (2002b) as follows:

> *self-centered welfare*: a person's welfare depends only on her own consumption and other features of the richness of her life (without any sympathy or antipathy towards others, and without any procedural concern). *Self-welfare goal*: a person's only goal is to maximize her own welfare. *Self-goal choice:* a person's choices must be based entirely on the pursuit of her own goals.
>
> (Sen, 2002b, pp. 33–34)

These kinds of privateness may be combined in different ways because they are independent from each other. For instance, when self-interested and self-regarding motives prevail, without any sympathy or antipathy for others, these three criteria are all satisfied (Hédoin, 2016). Those economic behaviors inspired by self-interest and self-regard are equated with the maximum of privateness because individuals forget public and/or social dimensions, mainly focusing on the maximization of their own welfare,[1] as in the standard neoclassical conception of economic agents and its atomistic assumption.

In contrast, a self-interested but partially other-regarding behavior satisfies self-welfare goals and self-goal choices but not self-centred welfare because some individual goals might be to improve others' welfare (Hédoin, 2016). A choice that violates self-centered welfare is: "one through which the agent actually derives sympathetic welfare" (Peacock, 2019, p. 114). This is what happens when individuals are dealing with someone who can feel sympathy.

Finally, when commitment prevails, individuals can even be totally independent of their welfare and/or their goals (Hédoin, 2016). In this way, privateness is erased. Commitment does not necessarily violate self-centered welfare, but it is able to modify individual goals and/or choices, respectively, causing a violation of self-welfare goals and self-goal choices. But we have to proceed gradually because Sen himself warned his readers that commitment "does not have (…) a unique interpretation" (Sen, 1985, p. 347), and this leads to different consequences on individual decision-making.

For instance, when an individual acts to "remove the misery of others from which he does not suffer himself" (Sen, 1985, p. 347), commitment can modify individual goals, violating self-welfare goals. It is important to emphasize that this commitment is accomplished without violating self-goal choice. In contrast, when an individual act of choice "is guided immediately by the pursuit of one's own goal (and, in particular, it is not restrained by the recognition of other people's pursuit of their goals)" (Sen, 1985, p. 347), commitment can modify individual choices, violating self-goal choice.[2]

Showing some differences between his and standard rational choice theory, Sen (1985) supported the idea that individuals do not lose their rationality even when commitment causes a worsening of individual welfare.

This difference is a conceptual possibility (but not a necessity) that is possible thanks to his notion of commitment, which explains how Sen concretely challenged the atomistic conception of economic agents towards a different understanding of individuals in economics. Furthermore, different from standard rational choice theory, Sen argued that commitment can be independent of preferences.

2.3 Critical perspectives on Sen's notion of commitment and the distinction between sympathy and empathy

In these last two decades, many economists and philosophers have written on the notion of commitment, probably because this is one of the most controversial ideas in Sen's works. According to Khalil (1999), commitment is problematic because individuals sometimes pursue this motive against their own interest, suggesting the distinction between 'binding' and 'non-binding' commitments to respectively identify those commitments without regard to interest and other commitments that take interest into account. Hausman (2005), instead, focused on Sen's concept of commitment compared to preferences, contesting his view that economists should recognize multiple notions of preferences. Pettit (2005) and Herfeld (2009) emphasized the clash between the altruistic attitude towards others that characterized commitment and standard rational choice theory. Building on Pettit (2005), Cudd (2014) successively highlighted the role of commitment in Sen's theory of agency, principally focusing on those commitments that violate the assumption of self-goal choice because they give rise to dilemmas, for instance, as compared to the standard philosophical theory of agency.

Then, Schmid and Peter (2007) edited a volume about how Sen challenged the issue of rationality underlying standard rational choice theory through his notion of commitment.[3] Finally, Peacock (2019) has recently devoted an entire monograph to the notion of commitment. In particular, Peacock explored the evolution of Sen's critique of standard rational choice theory through his notion of commitment. At the same time, he also focused on the ambiguities and weaknesses of Sen's concept of commitment, offering new, stronger interpretations of this idea. Adopting different arguments, what all these works have in common is an effort to critically analyse and/or further develop the notion of commitment in a rational choice theory framework.

In this work, we offer a further perspective on Sen's notion of commitment, exploring "which references" and "how these references" might have influenced Sen towards an alternative understanding of economic agents compared to mainstream *homo oeconomicus*. The choice for this focus is oriented to better understand the kind of economic agents Sen had in mind, given that he did not provide a systematic and unitary analysis of this issue. Based on a historical analysis of Sen's notion of commitment (and other works he wrote around economic behavior), we suggest that Sen was mainly influenced by Smith's notion of sympathy and Harsanyi's notion of imaginative empathy for elaborating an alternative, more balanced conception of individuals in economics where individuality and embeddedness coexist thanks to impartiality.

In this direction, we should primarily distinguish between the notions of sympathy and empathy. In several disciplines, 'empathy' is often confused with 'sympathy' because their respective semantics are extremely wide and have often been employed interchangeably (Fontaine, 1997, 2001). In the light of this still unsolved ambiguity, we adopt Fontaine's (1997) distinction, where sympathy "refers to the community of feelings, thoughts, and experience associated with a relation of similarity between individuals", suggesting closeness and resemblance among the agents, while empathy "consists in the process of imaginatively putting oneself in the shoes of another to understand his or her feelings, thoughts and experience" (p. 263), suggesting the separateness of normative agents.

Since the Fifties, empathy has become an analytical tool for helping interpersonal comparisons of utility in welfare economics, understanding others through imagination, without identifying with them. In this way, many economists began to understand themselves as impartial observers, such as *outside the group*, for realizing comparisons between individuals *in a group* (Fontaine, 2001).

Different from sympathy, empathy does not necessarily have a social dimension, rather a psychological one, limiting its activity to the knowledge of others' preferences instead of changing his/her goals and choices in the light of those of others in social interactions. Once clarified the distinction between sympathy and empathy, we might explore how Smith and Harsanyi probably influenced the origins and development of Sen's concept of commitment and his embedded impartial spectator through their respective notions of sympathy (in Section 2.4) and imaginative empathy (in Section 2.5).

2.4 Towards the embedded impartial spectator: Sen's interpretation of Smith's sympathy and impartiality

We have previously evoked Smith's notion of sympathy and his impartial spectator, stressing that his understanding of economic agents makes individuals and society finally connected. In particular, Smith also acknowledged the social nature of individuals in economic dynamics. This opportunity to connect individuals to society certainly sounds appealing to Sen, who was already trying to bring more sociality to economics by introducing economic motives like commitment that overcome the limits of the general notion of sympathy. For instance, the missing sociality. In an interview, Sen explicitly agreed with Smith that "the pursuit of individual goals in isolation may not be a sensible thing to do for people living in a society" (Klamer, 1989, p. 144). From this common element, Sen suggested that we might base individual behavior on individual goals and others. This quotation is a significant starting point that emphasizes a possible influence of Smith on Sen's notion of commitment. To show this influence, we should focus on Sen's interpretation of Smith's sympathy and his impartial spectator.

In this respect, Sen (2002a) introduced the distinction between closed and open impartiality, referring to Smith's impartial spectator. In particular, closed impartiality is about the procedure of making impartial judgments by the members of a focal group. In contrast, open impartiality is about the possibility of making impartial judgments without focal groups (Boran, 2005). Based on this distinction, Sen (2002a) argued that closed impartiality is that which we may find in Rawls's original (social) contract: "For the members of the focal group, the 'veil of ignorance' requires them to be ignorant of their exact identity *within* the focal group" (Sen, 2002a, p. 445); in contrast, Smith's impartial spectator is an example of open impartiality where "the demands of impartiality require the invoking of disinterested judgments of 'any fair and impartial spectator', not necessarily (…) belonging to the focal group" (Sen, 2002a, p. 446), namely the "distant voices" (Fraser, 2012).

Sen supported that Smith's strategy is oriented to override those partialities of group-based thinking that derive from a closed impartiality. This interpretation might explain why Smith argued in favor of scrutinizing individual sentiments from "a certain distance" to, on the one hand, avoid the influence of vested interests and question traditions and customs (Sen, 2010); on the other, better listen to those distant voices (Sen, 2002a). However, Smith (1759) further characterized the impartial spectator in terms of "abstract and ideal spectator" and the "real spectator". However, only this latter can scrutinize individual sentiments from a certain distance. In other words, the abstract spectator is the "man within the breast", characterized by weaknesses, like a child (Raphael, 2007), who is able to control their feelings only when others are present. On the contrary, the real spectator can judge his/her motivations and actions like a spectator because individuals also control feelings when others are not present, simultaneously obliterating self-interested motivations and behaviors.

Despite this ability to scrutinize individual sentiments from a certain distance, Smith's impartial real spectator always retains a social dimension because "in solitude, we are apt to feel strongly whatever relates to ourselves… The conversation of a friend brings us to a better temper" (Smith, 1759, p. 172). Sen greatly appreciated this open and social impartiality. However, Sen's view on Smith's abstract and real spectator has met widespread criticism (Bréban and Gilardone, 2020). According to Fraser (2012), Sen probably misunderstood Smith's dialectical approach to the abstract and real spectator, overemphasizing the latter. This misunderstanding might be associated with the main characteristics of Smith's real spectator, which influenced most Sen's concept of commitment (in particular, the effort to consider alternative moral motivations in economics and to control feelings without the physical presence of others). In this respect, Sen probably overemphasized the role of Smith's impartial spectator because he shared this *understanding of the impartial spectator* rather than offering a faithful reading of Smith's thinking. Indeed, the distinctive sociality of Smith's real spectator could have helped eradicate privateness, namely the same purpose that Sen intended to achieve through his concept of commitment.

2.5 On Harsanyi's concepts of imaginative empathy and impartiality: analogies and differences with Smith

Harsanyi is another scholar who might have influenced Sen's notion of commitment, although the analogies and differences between them are more controversial to analyse than those of Smith. In particular, we suggest that Harsanyi influenced Sen's notion of commitment through his notion of imaginative empathy. This influence is quite evident in some Sen's works, because there are also some passages where Sen directly acknowledged his debt to Harsanyi. In other passages, instead, this possible influence is more implicit.

A starting point for this analysis is the controversial debate between Sen and Harsanyi over their opposite position on utilitarianism (Erasmo, 2019). Albeit this significant difference, Sen (1977a) explicitly expressed his appreciation of Harsanyi's concept of imaginative empathy within this debate. I think that this point should not be underestimated. But we have to proceed gradually.

Since the Fifties, Harsanyi (1953, 1955) identified impartiality as a criterion that can realize interpersonal comparisons of utility. At the end of the Sixties, Sen joined a course about social justice where he had the opportunity to meet both Arrow and Rawls (Gilardone, 2015). On this occasion, Arrow and Sen "were parting company on the subject of interpersonal comparisons of well-being" (Baujard et al., 2014, p. viii). Although Arrow and Rawls were among Sen's favourite and most esteemed interlocutors of those years (Erasmo, 2019), they have very different perspectives about interpersonal comparisons of well-being: In particular, Arrow believed that interpersonal comparisons tended to be confused, while Rawls was sympathetic to primary goods comparison based on an index, excluding the idea of interpersonal comparisons of well-being in other cases. Among these scholars, Sen was the only one interested in defending interpersonal comparisons of well-being, violating one of the main taboos of welfare economics during those years. Meanwhile, Harsanyi had been working on impartiality and the possibility of interpersonal comparisons of utility for some years, availing of empathy. This element of his work could not fail to inspire Sen's curiosity.

But Harsanyi's impartiality was simultaneously indebted to some antecedents who also influenced Sen: on the one hand, Kant and his universalization criteria, together with the influences of classical utilitarianists, such as Bentham, Mill, and Sidgwick; on the other, Smith and his sympathetic, impartial spectator, a key reference – together with Harsanyi's imaginative empathy and impartiality – for showing their respective influence upon Sen's notion of commitment. At the end of the Fifties, Harsanyi (1958) offered an ethical theory where he tried to combine his view of moral rules precisely with Smith's impartial spectator. Significantly, Harsanyi recognized the strength of Smith's analysis of ethical and moral issues. However, Harsanyi preferred to use a small number of formal axioms in referring to impartiality instead of focusing, like Smith, on the simple change of positions (Fontaine, 2010). Although they both referred to impartiality, Smith and Harsanyi adopted different premises for their impartial spectator's judgments (Fernandes and Kandil, 1998). According to Smith: "the impartial spectator's judgment concerns a qualitative evaluation: the sympathetic perspective enables to experience others' passions analogically" (Fernandes and Kandil, 1998, pp. 147–148). In contrast, for Harsanyi, the impartial spectator's moral judgment concerns: "the fulfillment of impartiality criterion that qualifies this judgment and individual preferences through the empathic perspective that quantifies their content" (Fernandes and Kandil, 1998, pp. 147–148).

Based on this understanding of impartial moral judgments, Harsanyi suggested that individuals availed themselves of moral preferences, comprising those they considered rational, because these are evident when they force themselves to be impartial and impersonal, deciding to adopt a moral behavior (Harsanyi, 1979). Moral preferences differ from personal ones because they assign the same value to all preferences, including their own. Indeed, this mechanism leads to:

> imaginative empathy, on the ability to imagine ourselves to be in the shoes of other people. Of course, with the possible exception of some exceedingly unsophisticated individuals, all of us will surely realize that we cannot compare other people's utility levels with our own by merely considering the differences between their objective conditions (…) Thus, if I try to estimate another person's present utility level, then I cannot simply ask how much utility I would derive from the objective situations he is in if I had his taste and his personal attitudes.
>
> (Harsanyi, 1979, pp. 300–301)

Different from Smith, Harsanyi's identification with others is closer to empathy than sympathy. In this regard, Harsanyi was aware that understanding the utility someone achieves does not equal a differential between my biographical and biological existence and theirs: Rather, individuals have to imagine the utility they will achieve by trying to move from others' perspective, with their behaviors and personal tastes. This contrast is fully confirmed by introducing the similarity principle, which serves as an a priori formal principle for realizing interpersonal comparisons (Weymark, 2006). Based on:

> the basic similarities in human nature (i.e. in the fundamental psychological laws governing human behavior and human attitudes), it is reasonable to assume that different people will show very similar psychological reactions to any objective situation, and will derive much the same utility or disutility from it- once proper allowances have been made for any empirically observed differences in their biological make-ups in their social positions, in their educational and cultural backgrounds and, more generally, in their past life histories.
>
> (Harsanyi, 1979, p. 301)

So, people will have *similar* psychological reactions, but never *identical*: In fact, the biographical and biological grounds of every individual make the difference. The similarity principle has an *a priori*, not empirical, postulate, being provided as true by Harsanyi. He assigned this principle a value with the aim of incorporating it into rational choice theory. There is a double consequence: The similarity principle leads to impartial comparisons between utility levels in economics; in turn, this is instrumental to 'empathic' communication with others in the ethical field.

Consistent with this, the possibility of making interpersonal comparisons is a recognition that others have a real existence, as we do. Although there are individual differences, all human beings have in common an essential ability to achieve satisfaction or dissatisfaction (Harsanyi, 1977). Recognizing others' position inaccessibility inevitably requires that every instance has the same value.

2.6 Sen's reading of Harsanyi's imaginative empathy and impartiality

Directly confronting others' position of inaccessibility, Sen (1977a) wondered about Harsanyi's impartiality as a requirement of impersonality in ethical judgments: "Harsanyi's contribution in proposing his *as if* model was extremely valuable for what it taught us about the requirement of 'impersonality' in ethical judgments" (Sen, 1977a, p. 301). This is an important step towards Sen's embedded impartial spectator. Sen appreciated Harsanyi's concept of imaginative empathy as a virtuous elaboration of Friedman's *as-if* model. Unfortunately, Sen did not further argue about this theme in this or other works.

However, Sen (1977b) significantly wrote *Rational Fools* the same year as his "Reply" to Harsanyi. In this context, Sen (1977b) explicitly mentioned Harsanyi's (1955) distinction between ethical and subjective preferences that respectively permit "to distinguish between what a person thinks is good from the social point of view and what he regards as good from his personal point of view" (Sen, 1977b, p. 336). In addition, ethical preferences are characterized by impartiality because they express what an individual prefers "in those possibly rare moments when he forces a special impartial and impersonal attitude on himself". (Harsanyi, 1955, pp. 315–316). These elements show that Sen was also influenced by Harsanyi, mainly his notion of impartiality, for developing his concept of commitment, in turn, his embedded impartial spectator.

Evoking the distinction between ethical and subjective preferences, Sen (1977b) supported that his notion of sympathy enters into Harsanyi's understanding of subjective preference, while his notion of commitment might be associated with Harsanyi's ethical preference (Bowles, 1998), sharing characteristics like those of impartiality and sociality. However, as Davis (2003) wrote, "Sen went further" than Harsanyi and "supposed that individuals possessed distinct, incommensurable or noncomparable sets of preference rankings, with some preferences so organized as to express an individual's moral judgments and others organized to express an individual's self-interest" (Davis, 2003, pp. 65–66).

Thus, we might conclude that Sen's concept of commitment is influenced not only by Smith's sympathy but also by Harsanyi's concept of imaginative empathy through impartiality. Sen shared with Harsanyi the same interest to explore interpersonal comparisons (uncommon among Sen's main interlocutors of those years) and the need to be an impartial spectator to be an ethical observer. Although these elements are in common, the methodological differences between Sen and Harsanyi cannot be underestimated. The most obvious is probably their different perspective on utilitarianism, as mentioned above: Harsanyi was a leading advocate of utilitarianism; on the contrary, Sen was a leading critic. Another relevant difference is their opposite understanding of the relationship between social interactions and the knowledge of others' preferences. This different understanding is principally influenced by their respective methodological framework, namely Sen's capability approach and Harsanyi's utilitarianism.

Indeed, like Harsanyi, Sen considered needs under preferences as profoundly heterogeneous. In contrast to Harsanyi, however, Sen did not assign the same value to each. Despite the common recognition of this heterogeneity, Sen (1993, 2009) returned several times to the incompleteness of his capability approach, supporting the idea of the impossibility of reaching complete and total preference orderings (Sudgen, 1993).

In this regard, Hédoin (2016) emphasizes that we should distinguish two different kinds of incompleteness in Sen (2002b, 2009): on the one hand, assertive incompleteness, namely that incommensurability among different alternatives, which "cannot be compared along the same dimension making them ultimately impossible to rank" (Hédoin, 2016, p. 14). So, this is an insurmountable kind of incompleteness; on the other hand, there is tentative incompleteness, which tries to overcome the ambiguity of assertive incompleteness through partial but complete orderings, such as meta-preferences orderings, like in Sen's capability approach.

According to Sen, it is possible to realize interpersonal comparisons exclusively between meta-preferences orderings representative of the most relevant functionings (not preferences) for a dignified existence. This conclusion would not have been possible for Harsanyi (1955) because his utilitarianism was based on an expected utility theory that depended on the completeness axiom's meaningfulness.

Before analysing the relationship between social interactions and the knowledge of others' preferences in Harsanyi and Sen, aside from incompleteness, rationality is necessary. Although incompleteness rules out optimization (such as the possibility to choose the best alternative), but enables maximization (namely the possibility to choose an alternative that is not worse than the other available ones), incompleteness is consistent with rational behaviors (Hédoin, 2016).

Therefore, "the strong assumption that one must enter into a social interaction with an already complete preference ordering is unnecessary as a component of a theory of rational behavior" (Hédoin, 2016, p. 14). In this way, in Sen, in contrast to Harsanyi, it is possible to understand that social interactions might precede the knowledge of others' preferences without a lack of rationality of economic agents. Meanwhile, Harsanyi's knowledge of others' preferences becomes verified through imaginative empathy, which is, in turn, a requirement for social interactions.

This element confirms how relevant it is to consider the intellectual climate about interpersonal comparisons of the Sixties, based on Sen's initial interest in Harsanyi's imaginative empathy and its correlated impartiality that was progressively replaced by several methodological differences, for instance, to an opposite understanding of the relationship between social interactions and the knowledge of others' preferences. All these elements make Harsanyi's influence on Sen's concept of commitment more contentious than Smith's.

2.7 Concluding remarks

The analysis of the origins and development of Sen's concept of commitment suggested that, on the one hand, Sen's concept of commitment borrowed from Smith's sympathy for the same plastic strength of social interactions (namely that ability to change individual goals and choices based on those of others) and to be a criterion of moral approval and disapproval. On the other hand, drawing from Harsanyi's imaginative empathy, Sen recovered impartiality about moral preferences and an interest in interpersonal comparisons. But Sen's conclusion departed from Harsanyi with an opposite understanding of the relationship between social interactions and the knowledge of others' preferences. Their methodological differences mainly influenced this clash.

All these elements influenced Sen's concept of commitment, leading to what we define here as an 'embedded impartial spectator'. Characteristically, this embedded impartial spectator preserves his/her separateness from the others without losing his/her individuality (as in Harsanyi's imaginative empathy) but simultaneously acquires a social dimension, changing individual goals and choices based on those of others, as with Smith's sympathy. We conclude this chapter by stressing that Sen's notion of commitment enables us to talk about reciprocity in economics, one of the main concepts discussed in this book. This reciprocity is not the same as usually adopted in philosophy; rather, it refers to considering others' goals, choices, and welfare in economic decision-making. However, we will further develop Sen's embedded impartial spectator in the next chapters through its responsibility (in particular, through agency, as discussed in Chapter 4) and its missing mutuality (that might be, instead, recovered by the civil economy tradition, as we point in Chapters 5 and 6).

Notes

1 In particular, selfish behaviors are those someone has in mainly instrumental relationships, as he/she is oriented to an improvement of his/her individual welfare without taking into account of spill-over he/she produces on others' welfare. In perfect competitive markets, if individuals are self-interested, it will have the maximization of social welfare and perfect Walrasian equilibrium, in line with the fundamental theorems of welfare economics. However, given that informative asymmetry and control problems related to the subject involved are common, there is a worsening of social welfare (Depedri, 2008).

2 To better explain Sen's perspective about self-goal choice, Pettit (2005) introduced the distinction between goal-modifying commitment and goal-displacing commitment: the first modifies individual goals on the joint basis of the recognition of those of others and how individual behavior may affect them; the second is a motive that replaces individual goals with others' goals (otherwise, an impartial moral norm). Thus, only goal-displacing commitment violates self-goal choice.

3 The contributions in Schmid and Peter's volume

> fall into three categories. Those in the first part of the collection (…) revisit the argument of 'Rational Fools', with varying emphasis on the different steps of Sen's critique. The chapters in the second part of the volume focus on (…) the question of whether or not rational choice theory needs to be modified or abandoned in light of the possibility of rational committed action. Lastly, the third set of chapters discusses Sen's critique from the angle of collective intentionality analysis.
>
> (Schmid and Peter, 2007, p. 6)

References

Baujard, A., Gilardone, M. and Salles, M. (2014). A Conversation with Amartya Sen". *Social Choice and Welfare* (based on the 2010 interview at Harvard University partly online: http://www.unicaen.fr/recherche/mrsh/forge/262).

Boran, I. (2005). "On Distinguishing Between Types of Impartiality", *The Journal of Value Inquiry*, 38, 333–339.

Bowles, S. (1998). "Endogenous Preferences: The Cultural Consequences of Markets and Other Economic Institutions", *Journal of Economic Literature*, XXXVI, 75–111. www.jstor.org/stable/2564952

Bréban, L. and Gilardone, M. (2020). "A Missing Touch of Adam Smith in Amartya Sen's Account of Public Reasoning: The Man Within for the Man Without", *Cambridge Journal of Economics*, 44 (2), 257–283. https://doi.org/10.1093/cje/bez065

Cudd, A. (2014). "Commitment as Motivation: Amartya Sen's Theory of Agency and the Explanation of Behaviour", *Economics and Philosophy*, 30 (1), 35–56. https://doi.org/10.1017/S0266267114000030

Davis, J. B. (2003). *The Theory of Individual in Economics. Identity and Value*, London: Routledge.

Davis, J. B. (2009). "The Capabilities Conception of the Individual", *Review of Social Economy*, LXVII (4), 413–429. https://doi.org/10.1080/00346760903254250

Davis, J. B. (2024). *Identity, Capabilities, and Changing Economics*, Cambridge: Cambridge University Press. https://doi.org/10.1017/9781009438247

Depedri, S. (2008). "L'evoluzione delle motivazioni: altruismo verso egoismo nell'impresa sociale", *Impresa Sociale*, 81–102.

Erasmo, V. (2019). "The Foundational Decade to *Amartya Sen*'s Capability Approach (1970–1980)", *Rivista di Storia Economica*, 3, 295–336. https://doi.org/10.1410/98221

Fernandes, A. and Kandil, F. (1998). "Théories de l'Action et Normativité chez Adam Smith et chez John C. Harsanyi", *Cahiers d'économie politique*, 33, 137–158. www.jstor.org/stable/43111540

Fontaine, P. (1997). "Identification and Economic Behavior Sympathy and Empathy in Historical Perspective", *Economics and Philosophy*, 13 (2), 261–280. https://doi.org/10.1017/S026626710000451X

Fontaine, P. (2001). "The Changing Place of Empathy in Welfare Economics", *History of Political Economy*, 33 (3), 387–409.

Fontaine, P. (2010). "The Homeless Observer: John Harsanyi on Interpersonal Utility Comparisons and Bargaining, 1950–1964", *Journal of the History of Economic Thought*, 32 (2), 145–173. https://doi.org/10.1017/S1053837210000155

Fraser, I. (2012). "Distant Voices: Amartya Sen on Adam Smith's Impartial Spectator", *Culture and Dialogue*, 2 (2), 47–67.

Gilardone, M. (2015). "Rawls's Influence and Counter-Influence on Sen: Postwelfarism and Impartiality", *European Journal of Economics Thought*, 22 (2), 198–235. https://doi.org/10.1080/09672567.2013.792365

Harsanyi, J. (1953). "Welfare Economics of Variables Tastes", *The Review of Economic Studies*, 21 (3), 204–213. https://doi.org/10.2307/2295773

Harsanyi, J. (1955). "Cardinal Welfare, Individualistic Ethics and Interpersonal Comparisons of Utility", *Journal of Political Economics*, 63 (4), 309–321. https://doi.org/10.1086/257678

Harsanyi, J. (1958). "Ethics in Terms of Hypothetical Imperatives", *Mind*, 67 (267), 305–316.

Harsanyi, J. (1977). "Nonlinear Social Welfare Functions: A Rejoinder to Sen", *Foundational Problems in Special Sciences*, vol 6, 293–296. https://doi.org/10.1007/BF00136200

Harsanyi, J. (1979). "Bayesian Decision Theory, Rule Utilitarianism, and Arrow's Impossibility Theorem", *Theory and Decision*, 11 (3), 289–317. https://doi.org/10.1007/BF00126382

Hausman, D. (2005). "Sympathy, Commitment and Preference", *Economics and Philosophy*, 21 (1), 33–50. https://doi.org/10.1017/S0266267104000379

Hédoin, C. (2016). "Sen's Criticism of Revealed Preference Theory and Its 'Neosamuelsonian Critique': A Methodological and Theoretical Assessment", *Journal of Economic Methodology*, 23 (4), 349–373. https://doi.org/10.1080/1350178X.2016.1218530

Herfeld, C. (2009). "The Motive of Commitment and Its Implications in Rational Choice Theory", *Analyse & Kritik*, 2, 291–317.

Khalil, E. (1990). "Beyond Self-interest and Altruism: A Reconstruction of Adam Smith's Theory of Human Conduct", *Economics and Philosophy*, 6 (2), 255–273. https://doi.org/10.1017/S0266267100001243

Khalil, E. (1999). "Sentimental Fools: A Critique of Sen's Notion of Commitment", *Journal of Economic Behaviours and Organization*, 40 (4), 373–386. https://doi.org/10.1017/S0266267100001243

Klamer, A. (1989). "A Conversation With Amartya Sen", *Journal of Economic Perspectives*, 3 (1), 135–150. https://doi.org/10.1257/jep.3.1.135

Peacock, M. (2019). *Amartya Sen and Rational Choice: The Concept of Commitment*, London: Routledge.

Pettit, P. (2005). "Construing Sen on Commitment", *Economics and Philosophy*, 21 (1), 15–32. https://doi.org/10.1017/S0266267104000367

Raphael, D. (2007). *The Impartial Spectator. Adam Smith's Moral Philosophy*, Oxford: Clarendon Press.

Schmid, H. B. and Peter, F. (2007). *Rationality and Commitment*, Oxford: Oxford University Press.

Sen, A. (1977a). "Nonlinear Social Welfare Functions: A Reply to Professor Harsanyi", *Foundational Problems in the Special Sciences*, 6, 297–302. https://doi.org/10.1007/BF00136200

Sen, A. (1977b). "Rational Fools: A Critique of the Behavioural Foundations of Economic Theory", *Philosophy &Public Affairs*, 6 (4), 317–344. https://www.jstor.org/stable/2264946

Sen, A. (1985). "Goals, Commitment and Identity", *Journal of Law, Economics& Organization*, 1(2), 341–355. https://doi.org/10.1093/oxfordjournals.jleo.a036895

Sen, A. (1993). *Inequality Re-examined*, Oxford: Clarendon Press.

Sen, A. (2002a). "Open and Closed Impartiality", *Journal of Philosophy*, 99 (9), 445–469.

Sen, A. (2002b). *Rationality and Freedom*, Harvard: Harvard University Press.

Sen, A. (2009). *The Idea of Justice*, London: Penguins Books.

Sen, A. (2010). "Adam Smith and the Contemporary World", *Erasmus Journal for Philosophy and Economics*, 3 (1), 50–67. https://doi.org/10.23941/ejpe.v3i1.39

Smith, A. (1759). *The Theory of Moral Sentiments*, London: A. Millar.

Sudgen, R. (1993). "Welfare, Resources and Capability: A Review of Inequality Reexamined by Amartya Sen", *Journal of Economic Literature*, 31 (4), 1947–1962. www.jstor.org/stable/2728332

Weymark, J. A. (2006). *John Charles Harsanyi* (No. 0607), Vanderbilt University Department of Economics.

3 Self-sacrifice as a further economic motive for understanding Sen's view of economic agents

3.1 Introduction

This chapter adds a further layer to the analysis of Amartya Sen's conception of economic agents by exploring an additional economic motive that plays a central role alongside commitment, namely self-sacrifice. Both of these motives represent significant alternatives to the self-interested or self-regarding behaviors typically assumed by mainstream economic theory. However, while commitment is viewed by Sen in a mostly positive light, mainly for its potential to foster a sense of duty and collective responsibility in the face of socioeconomic injustice, self-sacrifice by contrast is generally regarded as a problematic phenomenon. It often results in a deterioration of individual well-being and is closely linked to perception bias, which can distort individuals' understanding of their own condition.

For these reasons, this chapter is specifically dedicated to examining self-sacrifice as an economic motive in its own right. Particular attention is given to how Sen, especially between the 1980s and 1990s, engaged with this issue in the context of development economics. During these years, he repeatedly emphasized the condition of women in less developed countries, where gender inequality is particularly pronounced and women's well-being is frequently compromised by behavioral patterns grounded in self-sacrificial social norms. In similar contexts, Sen argues that such behavior is aggravated by a perception bias, a cognitive distortion that prevents individuals, especially women in these settings, from recognizing the extent of their deprivation. This misrecognition not only reinforces social inequality but also poses a significant barrier to the expansion of individual freedom. By highlighting these dynamics, Sen once again broadens the analytical scope of economic behavior beyond the standard model of *homo oeconomicus*, introducing important cognitive and social dimensions into the discussion of individual decision-making.

In contexts marked by both structural inequality and cognitive distortion, Sen suggests that individual choices alone are insufficient to bring about change. What is needed instead is a broader process of public reasoning,

DOI: 10.4324/9781003381099-4

primarily a dialogic space where individuals can question, contest, and re-evaluate the social norms that shape their preferences and behaviors. However, this chapter privileges a focus on self-sacrifice as an additional economic motive to better understand the different possible forms of economic behavior within Sen's fragmentary but highly complex view of economic agents.

This chapter is structured as follows: In Section 3.2, we introduce the conceptual distinction between self-interest, self-sacrifice, and other economic motives, presenting the latter as a possible economic motive within Sen's framework. Section 3.3 frames gender inequality and perception bias due to self-sacrifice from a capability approach perspective, underlining the diversity of voices and experiences on this issue. Subsequently, in Section 3.4, we investigate how social embeddedness becomes a threat for individual well-being through the phenomenon of false consciousness, privileging the focus on the weakness of strong ties. In Section 3.5, we show how self-interest and public discussion are two possible complementary roots to mitigate the impact of self-sacrifice over individual well-being. Then, some concluding remarks.

3.2 Self-sacrifice: analogies and differences with self-interest and other distinguishing features of this further economic motive

In the literature on economic behavior, self-interest and self-sacrifice are often treated as opposing motivational forces. For instance, Overvold (1980) pointed out that the boundaries between the two concepts are more blurred and nuanced than they may initially appear. While self-interest is typically associated with the pursuit of individual welfare, self-sacrifice involves the voluntary acceptance of a loss in personal well-being. However, such a loss alone is not sufficient to qualify an act as self-sacrificial. Within the philosophy of welfare, self-sacrifice has been defined according to a set of specific criteria:

> i. the loss of welfare is expected or anticipated [...]; ii. the act is voluntary [...] iii. there is at least one other alternative open to the agent at the time of the act which is such that (a) if the consequences of the alternative had been as the agent expected them to be, then the alternative would have been more in the agent's self-interest than the act he actually did perform, and (b) if the agent had chosen to perform the alternative act, then his act would have been more in his self-interest, objectively, than the act which he actually did perform.
>
> (Overvold, 1980, pp. 113–114)

Based on this definition, Overvold argues that the simultaneous satisfaction of all three conditions is logically impossible. In particular, he agreed with Brandt (1982) that any behavior meeting the first two criteria is compatible with self-interest; thus, condition iii cannot also be fulfilled under a standard, unrestricted preferentist theory of welfare. This has led some theorists to conclude that genuine self-sacrifice is conceptually incoherent. Scholars such as Brandt (1982), Carson (2000), Darwall (2002), and Griffin (1986) have all advanced this position. Sumner (1996), moreover, interpreted Sen's (1977) early critique of the desire theory of welfare as an implicit endorsement of this conclusion, arguing that Sen aligned with the view that self-sacrifice lacks conceptual validity – a claim grounded in what Heathwood (2011) later called "definitional egoism". On the contrary, Sen admitted self-sacrifice as a meaningful, if problematic, economic motive, which is distinct not only from self-interest but also from commitment. Notably, Sen developed this line of thought not only in his theoretical work on social choice theory (e.g., Sen, 1977, 1985) but also in his writings on development economics throughout the 1980s and 1990s (e.g., Drèze and Sen, 1989; Kynch and Sen, 1983; Sen, 1983, 1987, 1989, 1990a, 1990b). This context-specific focus helps explain why Sumner may have overlooked Sen's nuanced treatment of self-sacrifice.

In his empirical and theoretical contributions to development economics, Sen explored contexts in which gender inequality severely limits individual freedoms, particularly in less developed countries. He paid special attention to the condition of women, whose well-being is often undermined by deeply internalized norms of self-sacrifice. Drawing on anthropological insights (Kapur, 1999), Sen reported that when rural Indian women were asked whether they considered themselves deprived, many responded negatively – not because their lives were objectively satisfactory, but because their frame of reference was their family's well-being, not their own. As Sen observed, "they didn't understand the question. They were talking about family welfare rather than their own individual welfare" (Kapur, 1999). In these cases, women's economic behavior appears to be shaped by a form of perception bias, preventing them from recognizing their own deprivation.

Through this lens, Sen investigated how self-sacrifice emerges as a behavioral pattern linked to both gender inequality and cognitive distortions. His position sharply diverged from standard economic assumptions, incorporating such cognitive elements into the analysis of economic agents. Crucially, Sen suggested that when self-sacrifice is driven by distorted perceptions and unequal structures, addressing these issues requires more than improving access to choices. It requires public reasoning and collective dialogue. These discursive processes enable individuals to re-examine the social norms guiding their decisions and to become aware of previously unrecognized injustices.

In this chapter, the primary focus is on self-sacrifice itself, considered as an economic motive. While public discussion certainly plays a vital role in Sen's later works, in particular, in relation to democratic deliberation and justice, this aspect will only briefly be mentioned in the concluding remarks, because the main focus of this book is on economic agents and economic motives. For this reason, the emphasis here is on the motivational structure of self-sacrificial behavior, its implications for well-being, and its position compared to other economic motives in Sen's framework.

In this context, self-sacrifice emerges as a distinguishing feature within Sen's view of economic agents. For instance, in his work on poverty and inequality in developing countries, Sen emphasized how these societies are marked by high fertility, poverty, poor health systems, and limited education, especially for women (Sen, 1997). Against this backdrop, Sen contributed to the early literature on gender bias in South Asia (Klasen and Wink, 2003), analysing the distribution of food, health, and educational resources. In particular, studies such as those of Lynch and Sen (1983) and Sen and Sengupta (1983) highlighted skewed sex ratios and gendered mortality patterns in countries like India, China, and others in the Middle East and North Africa.

What distinguishes self-sacrifice from other motives in Sen's account is that it is neither directed towards individual well-being (as in self-interest or sympathy) nor aimed at collective well-being (as in commitment). Instead, self-sacrifice is driven by concern for family welfare alone. This is especially relevant for the current volume, which seeks to unpack the plural and often overlapping motives that shape economic behavior in Sen's ideas. In this framework, family welfare can be seen as a third dimension, distinct from the more commonly discussed individual and collective domains. In prioritizing family well-being, many – especially women – may knowingly or unknowingly erode their personal well-being, without recognizing their deprivation. Moreover, unlike agents motivated by commitment, self-sacrificing individuals often lack the recognitional space and agency required to resist injustice. Their identity becomes conflated with the family interests, precluding awareness of themselves as autonomous moral and political subjects.

This erasure of personal identity is particularly salient in Sen's reflections on development. As he noted, "there was a sense for a while that development was a very hard process, and that people had to sacrifice. There was a lot of blood, sweat, and tears involved", even though "in the early, classical writings in development you find that it was always assumed that economic development was a benign process, in the interest of the people" (Kapur, 1999). In the harsh realities of less developed countries, development is not neutral – it is lived as struggle and loss, particularly for those at the margins. Importantly, Sen continued to emphasize that "development is not quite as harsh as it used to be" (Kapur, 1999), but the structural inequalities that enable self-sacrifice – especially among women – remain persistent. Quoting Sen (1987), he observed how "a typical rural Indian woman would find the question [about deprivation] unintelligible", and if she were able to answer at all, it would be "in terms of her reading of the welfare of her family". In such settings, "the idea of personal welfare may itself be unviable" (Sen, 1987, pp. 6–7). This is the cognitive distortion Sen and others described as perception bias – a key factor in understanding the persistence of self-sacrifice as an economic behavior.

Before examining more closely the relationship between gender inequality, perception bias, and self-sacrifice, the next section will offer a preliminary conceptualization of gender inequality through the lens of the capability approach.

3.3 Self-sacrifice between perception bias and gender inequality: a capabilities-based reading

Within the broader framework of the capability approach, a number of scholars have engaged with the issue of gender inequality. In his recent memoir, Sen (2021) recalls that he has always considered himself "a leftist, given his major commitment to the reduction of poverty and inequalities" (Baujard, 2022, p. 1007), including those rooted in gender issues in economics. One of the notable contributions of the capability approach lies in its attention to human diversity (for instance, about race, gender, age, ethnicity, sexuality, physical ability, pregnancy, and caregiving responsibilities), as Robeyns (2003) emphasized.

Following this premise, Sen (1993) contended that gender inequality is better understood by comparing, through functionings and capabilities, what individuals desire to do or to be in their life, rather than focusing merely on the resources or means to achieve them. This critique aligns with his well-known criticism of Rawls' (1971) emphasis on primary goods (Sen, 1980), even in relation to gender disparities. Furthermore, it reflects Sen's intention to provide a general evaluative framework, instead of a complete normative theory, through the capability approach (Robeyns, 2003, p. 62). As noted by Baujard and Gilardone (2017), Sen deliberately refrained from enumerating a fixed list of capabilities, as his approach retains primarily heuristic value for the construction of a theory of justice.

Some feminist economists, however, have concretely operationalized the capability framework for addressing gender inequality. For instance, Alkire and Black (1997) and Nussbaum (1995, 2000, 2003) proposed a universal list of capabilities that could serve to assess gender injustice, while Robeyns (2003) developed a context-specific list tailored to the analysis of gender inequality in Western contexts. These efforts suggest that both gender and geographical context matter significantly in shaping the relevant capabilities needed to assess women's achieved functionings and freedoms. As Robeyns (2003) notes, Sen endorsed the view that any list of capabilities should be context-dependent, shaped by both the geographical area and the evaluative purpose. Nevertheless, these structural dimensions, while crucial, are not sufficient to explain why certain individuals, particularly women in less developed regions, tend to adopt self-sacrificing behaviors. To fully grasp this phenomenon, the concept of perception bias must also be considered.

In his analyses of gender inequality, Sen highlighted intra-household distributions of basic capabilities, observing that access is not equally shared among family members (Kynch and Sen, 1983; Sen, 1983). In contexts marked by significant inequality within families, certain deprivations may go unrecognized by those who experience them (Gilardone, 2021). This is what Sen refers to as "perception bias", namely a cognitive distortion that prevents individuals, mainly women in traditional settings, from perceiving their own disadvantage. According to Sen's view of economic agents, individuals may, therefore, misjudge their actual state of well-being due to environmentally induced misperceptions about the capabilities and entitlements concretely achieved. In this regard, Gilardone (2021) identified three possible causes of perception bias in this context: (i) an exaggerated emphasis on male needs – especially those of the male household head (Kynch and Sen, 1983); (ii) a distorted view of each gender's contribution to household prosperity (Drèze & Sen, 1989); (iii) a socially constructed view of self-interest shaped by prevailing norms and values (Sen, 1989).

Among these, the first two causes are especially relevant for understanding the emergence of self-sacrifice as an economic motive among women. They contribute to the belief that men's needs are inherently more important, whether due to their formal role as head of the household or their presumed superior contribution to the household economy. To more accurately describe intra-household dynamics, Sen (1989) and Drèze and Sen (1989) developed the notion of "cooperative conflict" (Gilardone, 2021). According to this model, cooperation and conflict can coexist within family arrangements. In Sen's (1990a) work on gender divisions, he argues that cooperative structures, while seemingly harmonious, may perpetuate inequalities in the distribution of basic goods and responsibilities. As he explains, the outcome of shared activities (e.g. food allocation in poor households) can reflect underlying inequalities: "the nature of the co-operative arrangements implicitly influences the distributional parameters and the household's response to conflicts of interests" (Sen, 1987, p. 15).

In his broader reflections on gendered economic roles, Sen observed that family dynamics are fraught with ambiguities concerning individuals' interests and deserved outcomes. These ambiguities are often sustained by the diffusion of social technology, a term referring to institutional and cultural structures that relegate women to the domestic sphere and validate their secondary social status (Gilardone, 2008). While social technology may not be the only explanatory factor, it significantly distorts individual perception, especially among women. As Sen put it: Perception bias particularly impacts "the understanding of the interests of the others in the family that apply particularly to women in traditional societies" (Sen, 1987, p. 24).

This distortion of self-perception leads many women (and, in some cases, men) to adopt self-sacrifice in their decision. A woman, Sen writes, "may get a worse deal in the collusive solution if [...] her perceived interest takes little note of […] her own well-being" (Sen, 1987, p. 24). This neglect of individual well-being is a distinguishing feature of self-sacrifice as an economic behavior. While this section draws primarily on women's perception bias, it should be acknowledged that men can also follow self-sacrifice as a motive for action, particularly under conditions of extreme deprivation. A possible example recounted in Sen's memoir (2021) illustrates this point. As a child, Sen witnessed a severely wounded man, Kader Mia, bleeding in his family's garden. A Muslim laborer, Kader had chosen to work in a Hindu-majority area despite communal tensions, in order to feed his family. That choice, motivated by his role as a father and provider, nearly cost him his life "This example effectively shows that men are also willing to self-sacrifice for the improvement of their family's well-being, especially in countries where deprivation is most severe" (Baujard, 2022, p. 1008).

3.4 When social embeddedness becomes a threat for individual well-being: from the weakness of strong ties to false consciousness

While the early formulations of mainstream orthodox economics portrayed individuals as socially atomistic, Sen certainly challenged this view with his understanding of economic agents, thanks to commitment and self-sacrifice as alternative economic behavior. Indeed, these two economic motives mirror that the economic agents who Sen had in mind are rather socially embedded in the society they live in (Davis, 2024). In Chapter 2, we have already shown some limits of commitment. However, the case of self-sacrifice reveals an important limitation: When social embeddedness becomes too intense or restrictive, particularly in hierarchical or patriarchal settings, self-sacrifice can erode individual well-being rather than support it. In such cases, social identity dominates personal identity, and individuals may lose the capacity to recognize their own interests or to act upon them, in turn, worsening their individual well-being.

This phenomenon is clearly illustrated by what Sen called perception bias, a cognitive and evaluative distortion that affects people's ability to perceive their own deprivation, especially when self-sacrificing behavior becomes normalized within the strong ties of family and community. Thus, excessive embeddedness, rather than its absence, may become a threat to freedom and agency, on which we will come back with further details in Chapter 4. Perception bias, then, is not merely a psychological quirk, but a symptom of structural injustice. It reveals how socialization can internalize inequalities to the point that individuals are no longer able to identify or challenge their own deprivation. This dynamic aligns with what Marx (1978) identified with the concept of "false consciousness". For this reason, Sen (2002) evoked Marx and observed that false consciousness contributes to the persistence of injustice precisely because it results in "making allies out of the deprived" (Sen, 2002, p. 474; quoted in Qizilbash, 2016, p. 1212). Sen, therefore, turned his attention to those adaptive mechanisms that obscure the real conditions of inequality, mechanisms often embedded in both familial and societal structures.

Perception bias, as a cognitive distortion shaped by social norms, can be understood as a manifestation of false consciousness. In particular, it fosters conditions in which individuals, mainly women in highly unequal societies, internalize deprivation and embrace self-sacrifice without recognizing the erosion of their individual well-being. As Sen emphasized, in contexts where familial structures dominate, "the family identity may exert such a strong influence on [their] perceptions that [they] may not find it easy to formulate any clear notion of [their] individual welfare" (Sen, 1987, p. 6). This confusion undermines the development of a coherent personal identity. Unlike commitment, which enables for a dialogical interplay between the self and others (balancing individuality and sociality), self-sacrifice leads to a loss of self through complete identification with the family unit. This dynamic disrupts the equilibrium between personal autonomy and communal belonging. So, a proper social embeddedness should be rooted in commitment as a leading economic motive, but avoiding self-sacrifice as an alternative motive to self-interest.

For better understanding the consequences of individual identification with family, it is useful referring to Granovetter's (1973) and his distinction between strong ties and weak ties. According to Granovetter, strong ties, for instance, those within families or other close personal relationships, are emotionally intense and characterized by frequent interaction. Weak ties, in contrast, connect individuals across different social groups and are typically more instrumental, involving less frequent but more diverse interactions. Granovetter's core insight is that weak ties are more beneficial than strong ties for expanding access to information, resources, and opportunities, in particular, in labor markets or contexts requiring social mobility. In contrast, strong ties, while rich in emotional support, may entrench vulnerability by limiting exposure to broader networks, especially in underdeveloped or patriarchal settings (Erasmo, 2020).

Based on Granovetter's distinction, it becomes evident that the predominance of strong ties in women's social environments can exacerbate perception bias and hinder autonomy. When family becomes the sole reference point, the individual risks being absorbed by family identity, losing the capacity to perceive deprivations or improve individual well-being through the achievement of new capabilities. Thus, weak ties can serve as bridges across social groups, enabling forms of solidarity and reciprocity that challenge individualism without erasing individuality. In this sense, commitment fosters constructive weak ties, while self-sacrifice, especially in contexts of false consciousness and perception bias, deepens dependence on restrictive strong ties.

In many less developed societies, strong ties with the family dominate women's life, while connections with broader society are inaccessible or discouraged. This isolation has serious consequences: It inhibits the development of a self-conception beyond the family unit, thereby impeding the recognition of unjust conditions and the realization of basic capabilities. As Sen noted, when a woman "gets a worse deal in the collusive solution", it is often because "her perceived interest takes little note of [...] her own well-being" (Sen, 1987, p. 24). The internalization of inequality prevents her from asserting either individual rights or a collective identity that extends beyond the household. In other words, idealizing self-sacrifice as a form of "heroism", as happens in certain cultural traditions, risks legitimizing a system that inhibits individuals from achieving an acceptable threshold of capabilities. In these contexts, strong ties, far from being protective, can become instruments of constraint, obscuring injustice and forestalling the development of autonomous, socially embedded agents.

3.5 Self-interest and public discussion as possible roots to mitigate the impact of self-sacrifice over individual well-being

Sen was fully aware not only of the limitations of self-sacrifice as an economic motive but also of the structural consequences it entails for individual deprivation and inequality. To address these effects, he proposed two complementary strategies that operate on different but interrelated levels. On the one hand, within his broader reflection on economic behaviour, Sen suggested that self-interest, traditionally understood as the pursuit of individual welfare, could serve as a counterbalance to self-sacrifice. In contexts marked by deep inequalities, recovering a sense of self-regard may enable deprived agents to reclaim attention to their own well-being, often suppressed or overlooked due to social and familial pressures. On the other hand, in the more politically oriented dimension of his mature work (Sen, 2009), he emphasized the critical role of public discussion as a means to foster awareness, challenge adaptive preferences, and ultimately expand individual capabilities. However, we are currently privileging the focus on economic agents and motives, being the leading topic of this book, while we will come back on public discussion in Chapter 4. However, self-interest and public discussion may offer ideal pathways to mitigate or overcome the negative effects of self-sacrifice over individual well-being.

At the beginning of the 1990s, Sen introduced the now widely discussed concept of "missing women", emphasizing that more than 100 million women were absent from the populations of less developed countries (Sen, 1990b), particularly in China and several South and West Asian nations. The *ratio* of women to men in these regions appeared substantially lower than expected when compared to data from Europe and North America. This imbalance has been interpreted as a consequence of gender inequalities in the allocation of survival-related goods, which ultimately reduce women's life expectancy (Erasmo, 2023). As Sen (2001) later observed, "gender inequality is not one homogeneous phenomenon, but a collection of disparate and interlinked problems" (p. 466). Among these, he focused on what he called "natal inequality", which stems from cultural preferences for sons over daughters in male-dominated societies: "Given the preference for boys over girls that characterizes many male-dominated societies, gender inequality can manifest itself in the form of parents' wanting a baby to be a boy rather than a girl" (Sen, 2001, p. 466).

Based on the availability of prenatal sex determination technologies, the deeply troubling practice of sex-selective abortion has become widespread in countries such as China, India, South Korea, Singapore, and Taiwan (Sen, 2001). In his empirical studies, particularly those focused on South Asia, Sen drew attention to inequalities at the moment of both birth and death. These patterns are revealing and illustrate how some regions are more profoundly affected by gender inequality than others. In this respect, Sen (2001) warned

> Against the smugness of thinking that the United States and Western Europe are free from gender bias simply because some of the empirical generalizations that can be made about other regions of the world would not hold in the West. Given the many faces of gender inequality, much depends on which face we look.
>
> (p. 469)

If we limit our attention to birth and mortality-related gender inequalities, then, indeed, these are more pronounced in the Indian subcontinent than elsewhere. Between 1991 and 2001, the ratio of girls to boys under the age of six fell from 94.5 to 92.7 per 100 boys, with particularly sharp declines in states such as Gujarat, Haryana, Maharashtra, and Punjab. Kerala was the exception, showing a more balanced demographic profile. Although the use of sex-determination technologies for non-medical reasons was formally banned by the Indian government, this law has often been circumvented. This situation illustrates that the issue of missing women is not only about what others do to women but also about what women do to themselves, often unconsciously, after being socialized into self-sacrifice by their families. As previously explored, self-sacrifice is rarely a free and conscious decision. On the contrary, it is frequently tied to perception bias. These women are not only missing in a demographic sense but also symbolically, as their voices and individual interests are silenced through their own involuntary complicity in patriarchal norms.

This complicity, reinforced by perception bias, shows that when families encourage self-sacrifice, other household members may be acting out of self-interest, and commitment is disregarded because no one takes responsibility for preventing or mitigating these injustices. Based on this outcome, Sen has progressively suggested two complementary routes to counter self-sacrifice and improve individual well-being. At a "microeconomic level", self-interest, though generally criticized by Sen, can temporarily serve as a counterforce to harmful self-sacrificing behavior. At the macroeconomic and institutional level, public discussion can create the conditions for broader social change (Sen, 2009).

Quite surprisingly, Sen makes a concession because, when self-sacrifice prevails, it "is one of those contexts in which being more self-interested may do the world a lot more good" (Kapur, 1999). In situations of huge deprivation (such as those experienced by people who are used to self-sacrifice their own individual well-being), self-interest may become a necessary and even empowering economic motive. Although Sen is generally critical of self-interest as the foundational economic motive of the early formulations of mainstream *homo oeconomicus* (Giovanola, 2009), he acknowledges its potential utility when used instrumentally to protect and advance individual well-being. In such cases, self-interest is not a selfish act, but a rational response to systemic injustice, at least until broader, collective improvements can be achieved through public discussion and social transformation.

Subsequently, in his later writings, alongside with individuals' behavior, Sen (2009) assigned greater importance to the political dimension, through the concept of public reasoning, as a central mechanism for combating inequality and injustice. In this regard, institutions can play a crucial role in enhancing collective capabilities and implementing policies that reduce poverty, but they cannot succeed unless individuals themselves recognize their deprivations. That awareness can be fostered through public discussion, which allows people to examine and question their own situations. As Sen argues, when this process occurs, individuals are more likely to re-evaluate the distorted self-perceptions rooted in family or cultural expectations. By doing so, they begin to reclaim a more autonomous sense of personal identity and agency, which supports the development of their own capabilities and strengthens their well-being and freedom. For this purpose, Sen (2001) introduced the idea of "women's conscious agency" – a form of self-awareness that is essential for breaking the cycle of perception bias:

> This consciousness is important for women to overcome perception bias, but this awareness contributes to the lives of men as well as women, children as well as adults: [...] the greater empowerment of women tends to reduce child neglect and mortality, to decrease fertility and overcrowding, and more generally to broaden social concern and care.
>
> (p. 474)

Thus, improving women's conditions contributes directly to improving society as a whole. However, we will come back to the broadest general role of agency for Sen's understanding of economic agents in the next chapter.

3.6 Concluding remarks

This chapter has shown how self-sacrifice can be interpreted as a fourth economic motive within Sen's broader analysis of decision-making. Self-sacrifice differs from self-interest and helps better represent the diversity of real-world economic behavior. Sen developed his analysis within the framework of development economics, paying close attention to structural dimensions such as gender inequality, particularly relevant in the 1990s. By the 1980s, for instance, rational choice theory had expanded beyond economics, influencing fields such as anthropology, history, political science, and sociology, where it was used to explain collective behaviors like altruism, protest, voting, and organizational growth. However, a wave of criticism soon emerged. Scholars began to challenge standard rational choice theory primarily for its failure to account for individual heterogeneities and for its tendency to abstract from socio-historical and geographical specificities (Hodgson, 2012).

In this chapter, geographical specificities certainly play a pivotal role and Sen also considered these to include self-sacrifice in the discussion around economic motives. In the debate about the limits of rational choice theory, economic geographers were notably divided. While Miller (1992) accepted the rational choice framework, others – for instance, Barnes (1988, 1989), Barnes and Sheppard (1992), and Sayer (1976) – rejected both *homo oeconomicus* and the methodological individualism underpinning it. These authors critiqued rational choice theory's inability to consider the influence of place, space, and social interactions on human behavior. They also opposed the reductive emphasis on strategic rationality, in which collective action is reduced to a single dominant motive: self-interest. In contrast, Sen's contributions offered a significant extension compared to rational choice theory, introducing additional motives (commitment, sympathy, and self-sacrifice) that enabled a more nuanced interpretation of economic agency. Recognizing self-sacrifice as an independent economic motive enables a more accurate understanding of human behavior, especially in contexts marked by inequality and deprivation.

Furthermore, this recognition contradicts interpretations such as that of Sumner (1996), who argued that Sen even considered all forms of self-sacrifice ultimately selfish. On the contrary, according to Sen, self-sacrifice stands apart from self-interest, even if, in certain contexts, self-interest may function as a corrective to the harmful effects of self-sacrifice. This is particularly the case in severely deprived societies, where the promotion of self-interested behavior among women may temporarily serve as a means to improve their well-being. However, this should not be generalized to contexts where inequality is less acute. In fact, Sen's broader framework enables for a dynamic view of economic behavior that moves beyond rigid maximization models. His position is not one of ideological purity, but rather of pragmatic evaluation: He criticizes the overemphasis on maximizing behavior, but enables exceptions, like self-interest, when they are instrumental to human flourishing.

What might a "female revolution" based on self-interest, rather than self-sacrifice, look like? One key path, already explored by Sen (1996), involves reducing fertility rates by expanding female education. Higher fertility tends to correlate with lower literacy and employment among women. In contrast, improved education increases employment opportunities and reduces the economic necessity of having large families. As children are often viewed as sources of economic security (Abrams, 1997), voluntary fertility control becomes a crucial factor for female empowerment and improved well-being (Sen, 1994). Where this has occurred, such as in the case of Kerala, women's conditions have improved significantly, with broader capabilities made available through increased autonomy, employment, and smaller family sizes. In turn, the gender inequality gap can begin to shrink.

This perspective echoes the early insights of Condorcet (1795), who argued that high birth rates lead not only to increased scarcity, as Malthus (1798) claimed, but also to a direct reduction in happiness and living standards. A decrease in fertility, driven by education and self-determination, thus improves the quality of life, not just for women, but for children, families, and societies as a whole. Improved well-being becomes both the cause and the consequence of an expanded set of capabilities. Seen through this lens, lower fertility rates can be understood not as acts of self-sacrifice, but as expressions of individual self-interest, in the most constructive and transformative sense. They reflect not selfishness, but a recognition of one's own well-being as worthy of pursuit. They reveal, ultimately, that the path to justice and equality lies not in abandoning economic motives, but in diversifying and rethinking them. As the next chapter will explore, this transformation hinges on the notion of agency, an individual's ability to define goals and act upon them. It is through agency, supported by a capabilities-based framework, that we can offer a more complex overview on Sen's understanding of economic agents.

References

Abrams, P. (1997). "Population Control and Sustainability: It's the Same Old Song But With a Different Meaning", *Environmental Law*, 27 (4), 1111–1135.

Alkire, S. and Black, R. (1997). "A Practical Reasoning Theory of Development Ethics: Furthering the Capabilities Approach", *Journal of International Development*, 9, 263–279.

Barnes, T. (1988). "Rationality and Relativism in Economic Geography", *Progress in Human Geography*, 12 (4), 473–496, https://doi.org/10.1177/030913258801200401

Barnes, T. (1989). "Place, Space, and Theories of Economic Value: Contextualism and Essentialism in Economic Geography", *Transactions of the Institute of British Geographers*, 14, 299–314. https://doi.org/10.2307/622690

Barnes, T. and Sheppard, E. (1992). "Is There a Place for the Rational Actor? A Geographical Critique of the Rational Choice Paradigm", *Economic Geography*, 68, 1–21.

Baujard, A. (2022). "Home in the World: A Memoir. by "Amartya Sen" Book Review", *History of Political Economy*, 54 (5), 1005–1010.

Baujard, A. and Gilardone, M. (2017). "Sen Is Not a Capability Theorist", *Journal of Economic Methodology*, 24 (1), 1–19, https://doi.org/10.1080/1350178X.2016.1257821

Brandt, R. B. (1982). "Two Concepts of Utility". In Miller H. B. and Williams W. H. (eds.), *The Limits of Utilitarianism*, Minneapolis: University of Minnesota Press, pp. 169–185.

Carson, T. L. (2000). *Value and the Good Life*, Notre Dame: University of Notre Dame Press.

Condorcet, M. d. (1795). Esquisse d'un Tableau Historique des Progrès de l'Esprit Humain, Paris: Agasse.

Darwall, S. (2002). *Welfare and Rational Care*, Princeton: Princeton University Press.

Davis, J. B. (2024). *Identity, Capabilities, and Changing Economics*, Cambridge: Cambridge University Press. https://doi.org/10.1017/9781009438247

Drèze, J. and Sen, A. (1989). *Hunger and Public Action*, Oxford: Clarendon Press.

Erasmo, V. (2020). "Oltre le Specificità di Genere. Cura e Diritti nella Prospettiva Relazionale di Amartya Sen e Martha Nussbaum", *Società Mutamento Politica*, 11(22), 151–161.

Erasmo, V. (2023). "My Well-being Is (Not) as Important as Yours": Self-sacrifice as Further Economic Motive in Amartya Sen's Thought, *Research in the History of Economic Thought and Methodology: Including a Selection of Papers Presented at the First History of Economics Diversity Caucus Conference*. Emerald Publishing Limited. https://doi.org/10.1108/S0743-41542023000041B004

Gilardone, M. (2008). "Dobb, Dasgupta et Tagore: Trois Sources Méconnues de la Pensée d'Amartya Sen", *Storia del Pensiero Economico*, 2, 1–25.

Gilardone, M. (2021). "The Influence of Sen's Applied Economics on His Non-Welfarist Approach to Justice: Agency at the Core of Public Action for Removing Injustices". In Backhouse R., Baujard A. & Nishizawa T. (eds.), *Welfare Theory, Public Action, and Ethical Values. Revisiting the History of Welfare Economics*, Cambridge: Cambridge University Press, pp. 298–320.

Giovanola, B. (2009). "Re-thinking the Anthropological and Ethical Foundation of Economics and Business: Human Richness and Capabilities Enhancement", *Journal of Business Ethics*, 88, 431–444. https://doi.org/10.1007/s10551-009-0126-9

Granovetter, M. S. (1973). "The Strength of Weak Ties", *The American Journal of Sociology*, 78 (6), 1360–1380.

Griffin, J. (1986). *Well-Being, It's Meaning, Measurement and Moral Importance*, Oxford: Oxford University Press.

Heathwood, C. (2011). "Preferentism and Self-Sacrifice", *Pacific Philosophical Quarterly*, 92 (1), 18–38. https://doi.org/10.1111/j.1468-0114.2010.01384.x

Hodgson, G. M. (2012). "On the limits of rational choice theory", *Economic Thought*, 1(1), 94–108.

Kapur, A. (1999). "Human Development: An Interview with Amartya Sen". The Atlantic Online, December 15.

Klasen, S. and Wink, C. (2003). "Missing Women: Revisiting the Debate", *Feminist Economics*, 9 (2/3), 263–299. https://doi.org/10.1080/1354570022000077999

Kynch, J. and Sen, A. (1983). "Indian Women: Well-being and Survival", *Cambridge Journal of Economics*, 7 (3–4), 363–380. https://doi.org/10.1093/cje/7.3-4.363

Malthus, T. (1798). *Essays on the Principle of Population*, London: J. Johnson.

Marx, K. (1978). "Letters on Historical Materialism". In Tucker R. (ed.), *The Marx-Engels Reader*, New York: W.W. Norton.

Miller, B. (1992). "Collective Action and Rational Choice: Place, Community, and the Limits to Individual Self-Interest", *Economic Geography*, 68 (1), 22–42. https://doi.org/10.2307/144039

Nussbaum, M. (1995). "Human Capabilities, Female Human Beings". In Nussbaum, M. & Glover, J. (eds.), *Women, Culture and Development: A Study of Human Capabilities*, Oxford: Clarendon Press.

Nussbaum, M. (2000). *Women and Human Development. The Capabilities Approach*, Cambridge: Cambridge University Press.

Nussbaum, M. (2003). "Capabilities as Fundamental Entitlements: Sen and Social Justice", *Feminist Economics*, 9 (2–3), 33–59.

Overvold, M. C. (1980). "Self-interest and the Concept of Self-Sacrifice", *Canadian Journal of Philosophy*, 10 (1), 105–118. https://doi.org/10.1080/00455091.1980.10716285

Qizilbash, M. (2016). "Capability, Objectivity and 'False Consciousness': on Sen, Marx and J.S. Mill", *International Journal of Social Economics*, 43 (12), 1207–1218. https://doi.org/10.1108/IJSE-04-2016-0127

Rawls, J. (1971). *A Theory of Justice*, Harvard: Harvard University Press, https://doi.org/10.2307/j.ctvkjb25m.

Robeyns, I. (2003). "Sen's Capability Approach and Gender Inequality: Selecting Relevant Capabilities", *Feminist Economics*, 9 (2–3), 61–92.

Sayer, R. A. (1976). "A Critique of Urban Modelling: from Regional Science to Urban and Regional Political Economy", *Progress in Planning*, 6, 187–254.

Sen, A. (1977). "Rational Fools: A Critique of the Behavioural Foundations of Economic Theory", *Philosophy & Public Affairs*, 6 (4), 317–344. https://www.jstor.org/stable/2264946

Sen, A. (1980). *Equality of What?, Tanner Lecture on Human Values*, vol. 1, Cambridge University Press, pp. 195–220.

Sen, A. (1983). "Economics and the Family", *Asian Development Review*, 1 (2), 14–26. https://doi.org/10.1142/S0116110583000081

Sen, A. (1985). "Goals, Commitment and Identity", *Journal of Law, Economics & Organization*, 1 (2), 341–355. https://doi.org/10.1093/oxfordjournals.jleo.a036895

Sen, A. (1987). Gender and cooperative conflicts. Working paper 18.

Sen, A. (1989). "Cooperation, Inequality, and the Family", *Population and Development Review*, 15, 61–76. https://doi.org/10.2307/2807922

Sen, A. (1990a). "Gender and Cooperative Conflict". In Tinker I. (ed.), *Persistent Inequalities. Women and World Development*, Oxford University Press, pp. 123–149.

Sen, A. (1990b). "More than 100 Million Women are Missing", *The New York Review of Books*. 37 (20), 61–66.

Sen, A. (1993). *Inequality Re-examined*, Cambridge: Cambridge University Press.

Sen, A. (1994). "Population: Delusion and Reality", *The New York Review of Books*, 41 (15), 62–71.

Sen, A. (1996). "Fertility and Coercion", *The University of Chicago Law Review*, 63, 1035–1061.

Sen, A. (1997). "Population Policy: Authoritanism Versus Cooperation", *Journal of Population Economics*, 10, 3–22. https://doi.org/10.1007/s001480050029

Sen, A. (2001). "The Many Faces of Gender Inequality", *The New Republic*, 225 (12) 35–39.

Sen, A. (2002). *Rationality and Freedom*, Cambridge, MA: Belknap Press.

Sen, A. (2009). *The Idea of Justice*, London: Penguin Books.

Sen, A. (2021). *Home in the World: A Memoir*, London: Allen lane.

Sen, A. and Sengupta, S. (1983). "Malnutrition or Rural Children and the Sex Bias", *Economic and Political Weekly*, 18 (19–21), 855–864. https://www.jstor.org/stable/4372128

Sumner, l. W. (1996). *Welfare, Happiness, & Ethics*, Oxford: Clarendon Press.

4 The role of agency and capabilities in Sen's understanding of economic agents

4.1 Introduction

In the previous two chapters, we explored Sen's notions of commitment and self-sacrifice, which are useful for better understanding his conception of economic agents, here defined as the "embedded impartial spectator". This concept combines the distinguishing sociality of embedded economic agents (rejecting the social atomism characteristic of early formulations of mainstream *homo oeconomicus*) with separateness from others (maintaining impartiality in moral judgments despite social embeddedness). Conversely, we showed that "very committed individuals" can experience self-sacrifice, which in turn may worsen their well-being.

This chapter adds further elements to provide a unified view of Sen's understanding of economic agents. These elements are agency and capabilities. This chapter is structured as follows: In Section 4.2, we outline the intellectual context in which Sen (1980b, 1982) developed his notion of agency, namely social choice theory, rejecting both consequentialist welfarism and constraint-based approaches. For this reason, Sen introduced the so-called "goal rights system", which addressed the weaknesses of existing approaches to social choice theory. Subsequently, in Section 4.3, we emphasize the role of agency and capabilities within the goal rights system as a way to rediscover responsibility in economic agents' decisions. In Section 4.4, we further develop Sen's embedded impartial spectator by analysing his dualistic conception of the person in ethical calculation – combining agency and well-being (Section 4.5) – and by differentiating the embedded impartial spectator from partial mediators, such as those elaborated by Sugden (Section 4.6). This chapter concludes with some final remarks.

4.2 Sen's criticism of consequentialist welfarism and constraint-based theories: building the 'goal rights system'

Sen introduced the concept of agency[1] in the famous "Rights and Agency" (1982), although the term appears explicitly only three times in that paper.

DOI: 10.4324/9781003381099-5

However, in this first work on the notion of agency, Sen's discussion was clear enough to draw the role assigned to this concept from the very beginning. In particular, what emerges strongly is that individuals are not treated here as neutral economic agents, as in mainstream neoclassical economics during the 1980s. Instead, individuals are provided with "agency" that makes them ethically responsible for the consequences of their financial decisions (Erasmo, 2022).

In "Rights and Agency", Sen articulated his criticism towards welfarist consequentialists and constraint-based theories (à la Rawls), focusing on the proper relationship between rights and goals, halfway between social choice theory and moral philosophy. This focus helps clarify the theoretical normative context in which Sen introduced the concept of agency, another distinguishing feature of the embedded impartial spectator. According to Sen, these two approaches have in common to offer a poor or improper normative discussion of rights and goals. Using strong words, Sen claimed they were "fundamentally inadequate because they failed to deal with certain important types of interdependences present in moral problems" (Sen, 1982, p. 3). So, their limits are mainly related to the philosophical consequences of economic actions.

Regarding rights and goals, welfare consequentialists focused on the outcomes of individual actions, prioritizing goals in their ethical analysis of human behavior. In contrast, deontological theorists, particularly libertarians following Nozick (1974), emphasized the motivations behind human actions. According to welfarist consequentialists, "good" actions are those that achieve certain desirable goals. Deontological theorists, on the other hand, defined actions as "good" based on corresponding "good" principles, such as those inspired by specific rights, independently of their consequences (Cremaschi et al., 1996).

This classification may appear simplified to a philosophical audience, yet Sen (1982) adopted it to develop his proposal regarding the proper relationship between rights and goals. For this reason, it is useful to keep this distinction in order to provide a faithful reading of Sen's critique of these approaches, which ultimately led him to formulate the goal rights system, namely the normative framework within which the embedded impartial spectator should be situated.

In his analysis, Sen (1982) stated that consequentialism does not necessarily coincide with utilitarianism, apart from the same formal characteristics that make welfarism a special case of consequentialism. Not by chance, welfarism implies a consequentialist perspective in the moral evaluation of individual actions (including economic ones), expressed in terms of "useful consequences", whereas consequentialism considers "general consequences in themselves", not vice versa.

Questioning consequentialism, Sen (1982) also considered the consequences of individual choices, but including the ethical and moral implications, and avoiding the evaluator neutrality that characterized the early formulations of mainstream *homo oeconomicus*, often based on consequentialist welfarism (we will come back on this issue in Section 4.6, where Sugden questioned Sen's position about neutrality in moral judgments). In this regard, Sen (1982) aimed to overcome the traditional utilitarianism that prevailed between the 1970s and 1980s, which placed "happiness" at the center of the evaluation of individual welfare (Konow and Earley, 2008), by shifting the focus from utility or happiness to rights.

This hedonistic perspective, shared by welfarists, was the result of three specific elements, as Sen (1982) emphasized: (i) consequentialism, for which actions are evaluated based on the goodness (or not) of their consequences; (ii) welfarism, where the goodness of a particular state of affairs depends from individual utility functions; (iii) the theory of aggregate-utility, according to which individual utilities – expression of their individual welfare – should be summed for estimating the aggregate value of collective welfare (Ligutti, 2004) where it follows that the goodness of a choice depends on the degree of goodness of the deriving state of affair.

At the same time, Sen (1982) questioned deontological theories because they identified "obligation" as the only normative criterion in moral evaluation, in compliance with Kantian morality, avoiding possible influences exercised on individual decisions. Regarding constraint-based deontology, Sen showed that a theory based on constraints holds that the violation of rights is morally wrong, apart from the consequences. For instance, a better state of affairs for the members of a certain community that violates rights cannot be accepted because rights should always be respected, no matter the consequences.

Based on the inalienability principle, as in Nozick's libertarianism, the main theoretical difficulties are: (i) the exclusive link between moral rights and negative freedom (or the so-called "freedom from", namely the freedom to act without external coercion). If we assume that rights act as constraints on human actions, there is little room for positive freedom, namely the ability to achieve potential functionings, that is, the capacity to realize capabilities in certain achieved functionings or simply to expand capabilities. Sen (1982, 1993) considered both negative and positive freedom equally important in his pluralistic understanding of freedom, as we will explore further in Section 4.3. However, Sen slightly favoured positive freedom because it is more directly linked to the enhancement of capabilities (Erasmo and Santori, 2025). (ii) This strong connection between moral rights and negative freedom creates multilateral interdependencies, where restricting one person's rights may violate another person's more or less fundamental rights, thus generating moral dilemmas among claims with binding ethical and moral force. (iii) There is also the risk of counterintuitive outcomes relative to common sense, such as legitimizing crises merely because they arose within pre-existing rights.

Sen (1982) concluded that welfarist consequentialism and constraint-based deontology share a limit, namely the failure to recognize the moral rights sphere in evaluating the consequences of a specific action. In fact, the incapacity of rights to determine a social ordering, as Nozick (1974) notes, is the same as that of welfarists. For this reason, Sen (1982) elaborated on his goal rights system to overcome the further limitations of these two approaches.

4.3 The goal rights system: a space for discussing agency, capabilities, and freedom

In the light of these arguments, Sen (1982) offered his alternative to consequentialist welfarism and constraint-based deontological theories, combining those elements that he shared with them, elaborating what he named "goal rights system". In particular, this proposal was a consequentialist approach (as welfarist consequentialism) to individual actions without welfarist contents. Instead, Sen (1982) grounded rights for their intrinsic ethical value (as constraint-based theories) that finally offered a more complete normative dimension in economics, especially during the Eighties when the analysis of ethical and moral issues was in decline in economics due to the sovereignty of mainstream neoclassical approaches (Pettit, 1988). More specifically, the goal rights system considered the "fulfilment and non-realization of rights" as "included among the goals, incorporated in the evaluation of states of affairs, and then applied to the choice of actions through consequential links" (Sen, 1982, p. 15).

Thus, the goal rights system is a broader moral approach than consequentialist welfarism and constraint-based deontological theories, which might also be adopted by other normative perspectives on rights and goals. In this alternative normative system, moral rights acquire a double nature: On the one hand, they are measures of evaluative processes of states of affairs; on the other hand, the observance of these rights is both a means and a goal of human action for reducing inequalities and improving collective welfare.

However, the real novelty that Sen's goal rights system introduced to normative economics lies in the concepts of agency and capabilities. In this respect, agency and capabilities are distinct concepts, yet closely interrelated (Erasmo, 2023). In particular, Sen's concept of capabilities refers to "those beings and doings that constitute human life and that are central to our understanding of ourselves as human beings" (Robeyns, 2017, p. 39). Instead, agency refers to the power to act and the freedom to choose among possible alternatives based on individuals' preferences and values, without losing their rationality, even when the choices might potentially worsen their well-being (as in the case of commitment, discussed in Chapter 2).

In this theoretical context, where choice provides a seminal contribution to defining the nature of economic agents, Sen (1982) distinguished between positive and negative freedom. This distinction clearly evoked Berlin's (1969). In this respect, Sen (1982) did not explicitly draw this distinction; instead, he offered an interpretation of these two categories based on his pluralistic understanding of freedom, which also underlies his capability approach (Erasmo and Santori, 2025).

In particular, negative freedom means the 'freedom from', namely the possibility to act (or not) towards achieving certain ends without external obstacles. As in mainstream neoclassical economics, exercising negative freedom means having the absence of coercion because "coercion represents the impact of the behaviors and choices of others in limiting one's freedom, i.e., reducing one's voluntary freedom to volitional freedom" (Vatiero, 2013, p. 354). Negative freedom is a useful notion to highlight the environmental impact on individual well-being.

Conversely, positive freedom is the 'freedom to' be or do what individuals prefer in their lives, achieving (or not) those functionings that improve (or not) their well-being. Thus, positive freedom also implies self-determination in decision-making. For this reason, the concept of capabilities is closer to positive freedom than to negative freedom. Capabilities and positive freedom have in common that they refer to what individuals can concretely do or be in their lives (Sen, 1980b), while the environment's impact on individual choices should be associated with the exercise of negative freedom.

In his understanding of economic agents, however, Sen suggested that individuals should combine the exercise of negative and positive freedom to achieve their ends. Introducing the role of capabilities in his normative framework, where the impartial spectator elaborates his moral judgments, the goal rights system may be called a 'capability rights system' (Sen, 1982, p. 16). In his goal rights system, Sen elaborated a consequentialist, non-welfarist approach to rights that aims to achieve specific capabilities. Within the goal rights system, a goal right is synonymous with "a relation [...] between one person and some 'capability to which he has a right, for example, the capability of a person to move about without harm'" (Sen, 1982, p. 16). Thanks to this idea of goal right as relations, the distinction between "rights that relate to so-called positive freedom and those related to negative freedom, such as liberty and noncoercion" (Sen, 1982, p. 16) appeared more blurred. These nuanced boundaries make negative and positive freedom complementary rather than juxtaposed.

However, what is the link between freedom, agency, and capabilities in Sen's conception of economic agents? Individuals should combine positive and negative freedom to achieve the capabilities that might improve their well-being. Instead, agency is the power to act, representing the anthropological basis for combining these freedoms to make responsible choices among different capabilities, with the possibility of not maximizing individual well-being or questioning individual rationality for this (as previously discussed in Chapter 2). Exploring this point more in depth, agency enables exercise commitment as a rational economic motive. Thus, the combination of agency, capabilities, and freedom characterizes the goal rights system as the normative framework of Sen's economic agents.

4.4 "From agent to agency": coming back to responsibility and promoting collective well-being in economics

Focusing on the specific relationship between agency and the goal rights system, we can uncover the transition we define as "from agent to agency", which distinguishes Sen's understanding of economic agents from the early formulations of mainstream *homo oeconomicus*, who are an example of "economic agents without agency". In particular, through his embedded impartial spectator (primarily grounded on agency and the goal rights system), Sen advocated for responsibility in economic decisions because economic agents are not morally neutral, like in consequentialist welfarism and mainstream *homo oeconomicus.*

Sen's embedded impartial spectator is not morally neutral, thanks to his agency, which refers to a rational and responsible exercise of capabilities. This exercise is 'rational' because Sen (1977, 1985b) argued that motivations such as sympathy and commitment are equally rational than self-interested and self-regarding ones. Thus, the embedded impartial spectator may be guided by their own interests but can also shape their goals and choices in consideration of others' interests, thanks to commitment as the leading economic motive, as discussed in Chapter 2.

At the aim of reintroducing responsibility in the analysis of economic decisions, Sen (1982) referred to the notion of agency that leads to, on the one hand, the rediscovery of moral rights in the economy because they are the concrete expression of individual freedom (Sen, 1985c). This rediscovery of moral rights reinforces responsibility. On the other hand, considering others in economic interactions, thanks to capabilities, since individuals are regarded as ends in themselves rather than means to achieve goals, is an expression of relationality (Longato, 2017).

The goal rights system becomes a "capability rights system" for normative economics when 'wrongs' are functioning deprivations, while 'goods' are functioning achievements and/or the opportunity to actualize functionings as capabilities. In this way, the capability approach appears as a two-faced Janus: On the one hand, the capability approach explicitly acquires an ethical, in turn, qualitative value, through the goal rights system (understood as capabilities rights system); on the other, the capability approach conserves its economic nature, in turn, quantitative value, for estimating socioeconomic inequalities. The general idea of using a conception of individual agency (instead of well-being or human flourishing) is the normative ideal to select basic capabilities (Claasen, 2016), mainly in those socioeconomic contexts where inequalities are more evident. Basic capabilities are those capabilities that are necessary to have (a specific form of) individual agency.

So, Sen (1982) initially made the embedded impartial spectator a responsible economic agent by elaborating on the goal rights system, which we also discussed through related concepts such as agency, capabilities, and freedom. However, the link between agency and responsibility becomes clearer in his subsequent works, always dating back to the Eighties. Sen (1985c, p. 204) confirmed that actions coming from agency mirror the idea of individuals as responsible economic agents. Furthermore, agency is 'the moral power to have a conception of the good' (Sen, 1985c, p. 186). Different from the mainstream *homo oeconomicus* and its focus on individual welfare, Sen (1987) clarified that agency and well-being are distinct concepts. However, they are not opposites, since they are causally linked. In particular, agency might be oriented to individual, but also to collective, well-being because it refers to that ability to form goals, commitments, and values that can be "exercised at the individual level, or in groups, or through democratic participation" (Alkire, 2005, p. 219). Davis (2009) defined this ability as a 'self-organizing' activity that derives from the idea that:

> [A]gent's action not only affects the world, but also affects the agent itself through feedback effects that specifically individualize the agent rather than dissipate its individuality. That is, the agent's nature includes a particular kind of homeostatic feedback response mechanism that processes feedback from the world in this individualizing sort of way.
>
> (Davis, 2009, p. 416)

Well-being refers to the quality of human life, namely an individual achievement: how "well" is his or her "being" (Sen, 1985a, p. 5). Certainly, agency is not independent from individual success (understood as well-being) because they are intertwined. As Sen (1987, p. 43) notes:

> [A] person may feel happier and better off as a result of achieving what we wanted to achieve-perhaps for his family, or his community, or his class, or his party, or some other cause. Also it is quite possible that a person's well-being will go down as a result of frustration if there is some failure to achieve what he wanted to achieve as an agent, even though these achievements are directly concerned with his well-being.

In this respect, Sen stressed that individuals make good actions for themselves but also for others because, on the one hand, they are mainly inspired by commitment as economic motive in their decision-making (so, they also consider others goals and choices in decision-making and they can modify accordingly their own goals and choices based on those of others because they are, indeed, responsible); on the other, in turn, commitment as a leading economic motive refers to an understanding of economic agents based on choices and goals that often go beyond individuals' interests and can conflict with their own well-being (Crocker, 2008). For instance, commitment might lead individuals to help others affected by a disease, contrary to their individual well-being. For this reason, Sen (1992) provocatively claimed that it would be better to stay at home without helping those people, if we considered well-being only.

Including consequences in the analysis of economic behavior also lead to a rethinking of economic rationality. In particular, Sen (1985b, 1992) created the basis for stating that economic agents are still rational even when their choices lead to a decrease in individual welfare. Responsible economic agents might accept decreasing their individual welfare to reduce social inequalities without losing their rationality. It follows that the notion of agency includes responsibility and a rethinking of economic rationality. We will not explore the issue of economic rationality further because the literature is vast and rich. Instead, we will focus on the "dualistic conception of person in ethical calculation", the most complex expression of Sen's embedded impartial spectator through the concepts of agency and well-being/capabilities.

4.5 "The dualistic conception of person in ethical calculus": beyond the early formulations of mainstream *homo oeconomicus*

Sen (1987) further elaborated his understanding of economic agents at the end of the 1980s, consolidating the shift that we previously defined as "from agent to agency" (Erasmo, 2022), that is, from simply economic agents to individuals who also have agency (or responsibility) in their economic decisions and behavior. In *On Ethics and Economics* (1987), Sen returned to the agency/well-being distinction, referring to a "dualistic conception of person in ethical calculus", in which he included both agency and well-being to define what individuals are in economics (or, more precisely, he explicitly focused on the so-called 'ethical calculus', understood as the ethical and moral evaluation of economic decisions and behavior). In this respect, he argued that:

> There is an essential and irreducible 'duality' in the conception of a person in ethical calculus. We can see the person, in terms of agency, recognizing and respecting his or her ability to form goals, commitments, values, etc., and we can also see the person in terms of well-being, which too calls for attention. This dichotomy is lost in a model of exclusively self-interested motivation, in which a person's agency must be entirely geared to his own well-being. But once that straitjacket of self-interested motivation is removed, it becomes possible to give recognition to the indisputable fact that person's agency can well be geared to considerations not covered-or at least non fully covered- by his or her own well-being.
>
> (Sen, 1987, p. 41)

What Sen (1987) lamented is the unidimensional understanding of economic agents in early formulations of *homo oeconomicus* – based on a welfarist ethics – where individuals are mainly self-interested, in turn, focused on their own well-being. This "monistic understanding of person" is oriented to maximizing individual welfare, which often neglects agency and responsibility in economic choices and/or decisions. On the contrary, Sen (1987) showed that agency and well-being are two dimensions. However, agency might also diverge compared to individual welfare, for instance, when commitment prevails as an economic motive.

More specifically, in the dualistic conception of individuals in ethical calculation, Sen (1987) distinguished between agency and well-being, including economic motives beyond self-interest and selfishness. What is relevant in the dualistic conception of individuals is the understanding of economic agents in terms of their well-being, or, in other words, "a person's achievement: how 'well' is his or her 'being'?" (Sen, 1985a, p. 5), thereby acquiring a normative dimension. This point contrasts with the tautological formulation of well-being in mainstream *homo oeconomicus* (Sen, 1987). Indeed, whatever *homo oeconomicus* chooses contributes most to the agent's well-being, as it represents the alternative that maximizes utility, interpreted solely in terms of well-being and ignoring agency. Mainstream neoclassical economists thus espouse a monistic conception of the person in ethical evaluation (Erasmo, 2022).

However, Sen's (1987) criticism of welfarist monism (in turn, the early formulations of mainstream *homo oeconomicus*) is not just based on their missing responsibility in economic decisions and behavior, but also on the acknowledgement of a possible analytical mistake. In this respect, Sen (1987) stressed that welfarists did not realize that utility is not the reflex of welfare, but instead of agency. "Though utility is typically interpreted in terms of well-being, it is possible to argue that it might be better seen as reflecting a person's agency" (Sen, 1987, p. 44). During the Eighties, Sen further elaborated the agency/well-being distinction and suggested that individual well-being mirrors a person's agency. This new role assigned to agency within the dualistic understanding of individuals ethical calculus is confirmed in Sen's capability approach, as he argued that individuals' capability to choose what to be or do in their lives is based not only on preferences but also on values. Individuals' decisions are mainly based on preferences in the monistic understanding of economic agents, which undervalues the ethical dimension.

4.6 Distinguishing the embedded impartial spectator from partial mediator

Sen's understanding of economic agents as embedded impartial spectator has many distinguishing features: a well-defined normative framework, the so-called goal rights system that combines consequentialism without welfarist contents with rights; the reintroduction of responsibility in economic decisions thanks to agency, alongside the relevance to achieve further capabilities to improve individual (and collective) well-being, subsequently developing an explicit dualistic conception of individuals (where agency and well-being were distinct to each other) also to admit non-self-interested economic motives in decision-making. Now, we further characterize Sen's concept of impartial spectator through a comparison with Robert Sugden's mediator.

Both Sen's impartial spectator and Sugden's mediator represent two kinds of embedded economic agents, avoiding the distinctive social atomism of early mainstream *homo oeconomicus*. From their perspective, social relationships play a decisive role in shaping the identity of economic agents. Furthermore, Sen and Sugden share an adherence to liberalism and a willingness to promote interdisciplinary dialogue between economics and philosophy, along with a critique of mainstream neoclassical economics and a rejection of the orthodoxy of mainstream welfare economics (Hunt and Stanley, 2019). In particular, Sen and Sugden rejected the assumption that individual choices, desires (happiness and pleasure), and preferences should serve as the basis for evaluating and judging social states, since these concepts are fundamentally welfarist.

However, based on this common refusal, they adopted a different normative framework to overcome utilitarianism and its missing consideration for issues like freedom and opportunities. The relevance of this comparison between Sen (2006, 2008, 2009) and Sugden (1985, 1993, 2006, 2008, 2018) is that they established a dialogue (partially explicit, partially implicit) on their respective ideas of what normative economics should be, not only focusing on their views of the market but also on the economist's role[2] (Erasmo and Santori, 2025).

For the purposes of this book, we will focus on this second point. In particular, Sugden stressed that Sen was in favour of an impartial economist, whereas he endorsed the idea that economists are non-neutral mediators. He criticized Sen for including impartiality in moral judgments, arguing that it is closer to a welfarist understanding of economic agents. Therefore, the Sen–Sugden debate in normative economics is relevant for offering further insights into Sen's understanding of economic agents.

According to Sugden, a liberal economist, by definition, cannot consider himself a neutral or impartial spectator, unlike Sen. To support this claim, Sugden did not focus on Sen's early works, as we did in this book. Instead, Sugden privileged Sen's later works, notably a symposium published in the philosophical journal *Utilitas* (2006) devoted to liberal scholars like Mill and Sen. In his contribution, Sugden (2006) stressed how he was personally sympathetic to a contractarian view of liberalism because it was an alternative to Sen and Mill's liberalism, which was instead based on a "utilitarian's view of the moral world" (p.34). So, Sugden (2006) associated Sen with that same welfarism he criticized since his early works, leading him to elaborate a goal rights system, a consequentialist approach to rights, explicitly without welfarist contents.

According to Sugden (2006, p. 36), instead, utilitarianism was the normative basis for Sen's "'moral observer' that makes 'judgements', 'assessments', or 'evaluations' of a person's state from outside". This chapter provided much evidence to show how Sen was skeptical of welfarism. However, Sugden (2006) emphasizes how the idea of a moral observer was grounded on an external analysis of individuals' conditions that certainly requires a certain degree of impartiality, which is, in turn, close to that same welfarist contents that Sen criticized.

Sen (1980a) confirmed this endorsement of economic agents' impartiality, for instance, through his skepticism towards subjectivity in economic descriptions in his early works. In this regard, Sen argued that happiness and desires, which belong to subjective experiences, do not provide a strong basis for moral judgments because economic agents are often affected by perception bias (Erasmo, 2023). Indeed, there are unhappy or deprived individuals (or even groups) who are unaware of their conditions (Gilardone, 2021) and do not aspire to improve their well-being. Discussing the limits of perception bias, Sen (1992) maintained that a subjective informational basis is ineffective for developing impartial moral judgments. This position encouraged the adoption of an objective positionality, an issue he further developed in his later works (Sen, 2009).

In this respect, Sen (2009) always endorsed the dialogue between economics and philosophy, particularly ethics and morality. However, Sen assigned a more nuanced role to values, especially in the social justice space, to strengthen the political debate promoting social embeddedness. In this context, Sen (2009) identified public reasoning as "an essential feature of objectivity in political and ethical beliefs" (Sen, 2009, p. 44) to identify just states of affairs. So, Sen's economic agents join public reasoning to confirm social embeddedness and ensure impartiality in moral judgments (and other evaluations of states of affairs) through an objective positionality.

Despite efforts to safeguard social embeddedness in economics, Sugden rejected this impartiality in Sen's normative economics, arguing that Sen was potentially a utilitarian economist, given the kind of economists he had in mind. Subsequently, Sugden (2008) added further arguments to support this thesis, analysing the limits of capabilities for well-being evaluations. During the 1990s, Sen (1992) pointed out that writing a list of capabilities to perform total and complete comparisons of well-being was impossible, as individuals can also disagree about well-being assessments. Sugden (2008) argued that this inherent incompleteness of Sen's capability approach stems from that objective yet vague notion of well-being, which reinforces Sen's (2006) endorsement of public reasoning (Baujard and Gilardone, 2017) to achieve "objectivity" in moral judgments.

At the same time, Sugden (2006) also rejected Sen's claim that economists, as ethical theorists, have better tools than other individuals to determine what is best for society. Thus, in public reasoning, economists would be more authoritative than others, according to Sen (2009). Sugden (2008) partially agreed with Sen that economists may understand human desires better than others. However, he warned that this creates the risk that they could directly "influence the assignment of freedoms in society" (p. 306), thereby threatening liberalism. In other words, Sugden emphasized the importance of safeguarding individual freedoms within collective processes, such as public reasoning and discussion, and critiqued the absolute impartiality of Sen's moral observer. For this reason, Sugden (2018) advocated the role of a mediator:

> who acts in good faith will look for an agreement that she can recommend to both parties as the best that each can hope to achieve, given that the other must agree too. Since it is evidence of good faith that her recommendations to each party can be stated openly to both, one might say that a good mediator is engaged in a kind of public reasoning. But it is a form of reasoning that recognizes the separate interests of the parties; it takes account of what is good for each party, from its own point of view, without needing to consider what is simply good, as viewed from nowhere
>
> (pp. 38–39)

Interestingly, Sugden (2018) refused the so-called "view from nowhere" shared by Smith and Sen, in favor of a public discussion where the separate interests of the parties are acknowledged. In particular, Sugden believed that all liberal economists, in general, should refuse views from nowhere (Nagel, 1989). However, the point is even more complex here and not limited to how a liberal economist should be. Sugden (2018) substantially believed in market superiority for promoting well-being in a society based on the idea of "mutual advantage" within market interactions and dynamics, instead of advocating for moral observers for that purpose.

For this reason, Sugden believed that

> economists should refuse every objective or impartial point of view. They need to act as mediators between contracting parties, helping them set the general rules of their agreement but not judging their individual preferences at any level. Mutual advantage is not what is best for the contracting parties from an objective point of view but what they deem to be good for them as compared to a situation in which the mutual advantage reached by the contract is not reached.
>
> (Erasmo and Santori, 2025, p. 867)

Apart from these different points of view, Sen and Sugden have the common purpose of improving collective well-being in economics based on social embeddedness in economic dynamics. Sen believed that the impartial spectator should be committed to this purpose, engaging public reasoning thanks to (an objective) positionality. Conversely, Sugden considered the markets to have a privileged role for mutual advantage, which improves collective well-being for reducing inequalities.

4.7 Concluding remarks

After the previous analysis of the notion of commitment as the leading economic motive, we completed the discussion of the distinguishing features of Sen's understanding of economic agents as embedded impartial spectators through the notions of agency and capabilities, as well as the role of freedom (negative and positive), the reintroduction of responsibility in economic decisions, and the willingness to improve collective well-being. Among these notions, agency and well-being are probably the most relevant, also from a socioeconomic perspective, because they provide the ideal conditions for reducing persistent socioeconomic inequalities in both more advanced economies and less developed countries.

Economic agents who incorporate others into their goals and choices (for instance, through commitment) can make decisions that contribute to building collective well-being, not only individual well-being, alongside policymakers' strategies. These features make Sen's understanding of economic agents relevant beyond the domain of the history of economic thought and methodology. We concluded this chapter by distinguishing Sen's embedded economic agents from those elaborated by Sugden, including his critique of the impartiality of Sen's moral observer, which paradoxically could bring him closer to the same welfarism he had strongly rejected since his early works. Thus, Sen's understanding of economic agents presents some possible theoretical weaknesses compared to his broader positions and to other contemporary scholars' ideas.

However, there is another point that Sugden did not further develop, which represents an additional potential limitation of Sen's embedded impartial spectator. This limitation does not concern impartiality, but rather embeddedness. Indeed, what is missing in Sen's understanding of economic agents is mutuality – the same mutuality that Sugden placed at the basis of his view of the market. In one of his later works, *The Course of Recognition*, Ricoeur (2004) emphasized the anthropological value of Sen's capability approach in elaborating a conception of economic agents that includes the social dimension, particularly social relationships that counteracted the general trend of mainstream neoclassical economics between the Eighties and the Nineties. At the same time, Ricoeur (2004) lamented the absence of mutuality in social relationships based on Sen's understanding of economic agents, particularly regarding his concepts of agency and social capabilities. We will explore Ricoeur's criticism of the embedded impartial spectator more thoroughly in Chapter 5.

Notes

1 For a broad discussion about agency and social choice theory, see Comim et al. (2024).
2 This subsection is deeply rooted upon an already published paper, namely Erasmo and Santori (2025).

References

Alkire, S. (2005). "Subjective Quantitative Studies in Human Agency", *Social Indicators Research*, 74 (1), 217–260. https://doi.org/10.1007/s11205-005-6525-0

Baujard, A. and Gilardone, M. (2017). "Sen Is Not a Capability Theorist", *Journal of Economic Methodology*, 24 (1), 1–19. https://doi.org/10.1080/1350178X.2016.1257821

Berlin, I. (1969). *Four Essays on Liberty*, Oxford: Oxford University Press.

Claasen, R. (2016). "An Agency-Based Capability Theory of Justice", *European Journal of Philosophy*, 25 (4), 1279–1304. https://doi.org/10.1111/ejop.12195

Comim, F., Anand, P. B. and Fennell, S. (eds.) (2024). *Social Choice, Agency, Inclusiveness and Capabilities*, Cambridge: Cambridge University Press.

Cremaschi, S. (1996). "Consequenzialismo e deontologismo". In Melchiorre, V., Boffi, G., Garin, E., Bausola, A., Berti, E., Castellani, F., et al. (eds.), *Enciclopedia della Filosofia e delle Scienze Umane*, Novara: De Agostini, p. 173.

Crocker, D. A. (2008). *Ethics of Global Development: Agency, Capability, and Deliberative Democracy*, Cambridge: Cambridge University Press.

Davis, J. B. (2009). "The Capabilities Conception of the Individual", *Review of Social Economy*, LXVII (4), 413–429. https://doi.org/10.1080/00346760903254250

Erasmo, V. (2022). "Amartya Sen's Earlier Conception of Economic Agents Through the Origins and Development of His Capability Approach (1970–1993)", *Erasmus Journal of Philosophy and Economics*, 15 (1), 184–193. https://doi.org/10.23941/ejpe.v15i1.596

Erasmo, V. (2023). "My Well-being is (Not) as Important as Yours": Self-sacrifice as Further Economic Motive in Amartya Sen's Thought, *Research in the History of Economic Thought and Methodology: Including a Selection of Papers Presented at the First History of Economics Diversity Caucus Conference*. Emerald Publishing Limited. https://doi.org/10.1108/S0743-41542023000041B004

Erasmo, V. (2025). "Extending the Capabilities Conception of the Individual in Economics: Relationality and Responsibility", *Journal of Interdisciplinary Economics*, 37 (1), 25–41. https://doi.org/10.1177/02601079231179372.

Erasmo, V. and Santori, P. (2025). "What Should a Liberal Economist (Not) Do? Sen–Sugden Debate on Welfare Economics", *Cambridge Journal of Economics*, 49 (4), 849–872. https://doi.org/10.1093/cje/beaf023

Gilardone, M. (2021). "The Influence of Sen's Applied Economics on His Non-Welfarist Approach to Justice: Agency at the Core of Public Action for Removing Injustices". In Backhouse R., Baujard A. and Nishizawa T. (eds.), *Welfare Theory, Public Action, and Ethical Values. Revisiting the History of Welfare Economics*, Cambridge: Cambridge University Press, pp. 298–320.

Hunt, T. and Stanley, L. (2019). "From 'There Is No Alternative'to 'Maybe There Are Alternatives': Five Challenges to Economic Orthodoxy after the Crash", *The Political Quarterly*, 90 (3), 479–487. https://doi.org/10.1111/1467-923X.12707

Konow, J. and Earley, J. (2008). "The Hedonistic Paradox: Is *Homo Economicus* Happier?, *Journal of Public Economics*, 92 (1–2), 1–33. https://doi.org/10.1016/j.jpubeco.2007.04.006

Ligutti, P. (2004). "I diritti come fini. La riflessione di Amartya Sen tra consequenzialismo e teorie deontologiche", *Filosofia Politica*, 3, 461–482. https://doi.org/10.1416/16276

Longato, F. (2017). "Agency e Relazionalità nel Capability Approach di Amartya Sen", *Esercizi filosofici*, 12 (1), 170–202.

Nagel, T. (1989). *The View from Nowhere*, Oxford: Oxford University Press.

Nozick, R. (1974). *Anarchy, State and Utopia*, Oxford: Blackwell.

Pettit, P. (1988). "The Consequentialist can Recognise Rights", *The Philosophical Quarterly (1950-)*, 38(150), 42–55. https://doi.org/10.2307/2220266

Ricoeur, P. (2004). *The Course of Recognition*, Harvard: Harvard University Press.

Robeyns, I. (2017). *Wellbeing, Freedom and Social Justice: The Capability Approach Re-Examined*, Open book publishers.

Sen, A. (1977). "Rational Fools: A Critique of the Behavioural Foundations of Economic Theory", *Philosophy &Public Affairs*, 6 (4), 317–344.

Sen, A. (1980a). "Description as Choice", *Oxford Economic Papers*, 32 (3), 353–369. https://doi.org/10.1093/oxfordjournals.oep.a041484

Sen, A. (1980b). *Equality of What?, Tanner Lecture on Human Values*, vol. 1, Cambridge, Cambridge University Press, pp. 195–220

Sen, A. (1982). "Rights and Agency", *Philosophy and Public Affairs*, 11 (1), 3–39, https://www.jstor.org/stable/2265041

Sen, A. (1985a). *Commodities and Capabilities*, Amsterdam: North Holland.

Sen, A. (1985b). "Goals, Commitment and Identity", *Journal of Law, Economics & Organization*, 1 (2), 341–355. https://doi.org/10.1093/oxfordjournals.jleo.a036895

Sen, A. (1985c). "Well-Being, Agency and Freedom. The Dewey Lectures, 1984", *The Journal of Philosophy*, 82, 169–221.

Sen, A. (1987). *On Ethics and Economics*, Oxford: Basil Blackwell.

Sen, A. (1992). *Inequality Rexamined*, Oxford: Clarendon Press.

Sen, A. (1993). "Markets and Freedoms: Achievements and Limitations of the Market Mechanism in Promoting Individual Freedoms", *Oxford Economic Papers*, 45 (4), 519–541. https://doi.org/10.1093/oxfordjournals.oep.a042106

Sen, A. (2006). "Reason, Freedom and Well-Being", *Utilitas*, 18 (1), 80–96. https://doi.org/10.1017/S0953820805001846

Sen, A. (2008). "The Economics of Happiness and Capabilities". In Bruni, L., Comim, F. and Pugno, M. (eds.), *Capabilities and Happiness*, Oxford: Oxford University Press, pp. 16–27.

Sen, A. (2009). *The Idea of Justice*, Cambridge: Harvard University Press.

Sugden, R. (1985). "Liberty, Preference and Choice", *Economics and Philosophy*, 1 (2), 213–229.

Sugden, R. (1993). "Welfare, Resources, and Capabilities: A Review of Inequality Reexamined by Amartya Sen", *Journal of Economic Literature*, 31 (4), 1947–62. https://www.jstor.org/stable/2728332

Sugden, R. (2006). "What We Desire, What We Have Reason to Desire, Whatever We Might Desire: Mill and Sen on the Value of Opportunity", *Utilitas*, 18 (1), 33–51. https://doi.org/10.1017/S0953820805001810

Sugden, R. (2008). "Capability, Happiness and Opportunity". In Bruni, L., Comim, F. and Pugno, M. (eds.), *Capabilities and Happiness*, Oxford: Oxford University Press, pp. 299–322.

Sugden, R. (2018). *The Community of Advantage: A Behavioural Economist's Defence of the Market*, Oxford: Oxford University Press.

Vatiero, M. (2013). "Positional Goods and Robert Lee Hale's Legal Economics", *Journal of Institutional Economics*, 9 (3), 351–362. https://doi.org/10.1017/S1744137413000076

5 Embeddedness without mutuality

Ricoeur's debt and criticism of Sen's understanding of economic agents

5.1 Introduction

After having completed the overview of the distinguishing features of Sen's understanding of economic agents, it is time to focus on the potentialities and limits of this conception of individuals in economics. As previously anticipated, in his latest works, Ricoeur (2004, 2006) discussed the missing mutuality in Sen's view of economic agents – based on his capability approach – which highlights potential ambiguities of the embedded impartial spectator analysed here. However, Ricoeur stood halfway between criticism and debt to Sen and his capability approach, elaborating a complex reading that deserves to be explored in a full chapter because it is useful for gaining a more complete picture of Sen's fragmented view of economic agents.

If Ricoeur criticized this missing mutuality, he also appreciated that Sen returned to the social dimension in representing economic agents, drawing on Smith's notions of sympathy and impartiality. In this respect, the strength of Ricoeur's reading of this social embeddedness is twofold: On the one hand, it shows how an important contemporary moral philosopher emphasized Sen's effort to return to sociality in economics, while mainstream neoclassical economics weakened the role of social relationships in the discipline in promoting social atomism. On the other hand, Ricoeur (2004) even acknowledged his debt to Sen for the importance he assigned to social relationships and translated this same effort into a philosophical context. Thanks to Ricoeur's "mixed" criticism and debt to Sen, we can better discuss why his understanding of economic agents is characterized by social embeddedness without mutuality.

An interesting literature on the relationship between Ricoeur and Sen already exists, and there are two main schools of thought. On the one hand, there are scholars mainly focused on Ricoeur's debt to Sen; see Brugiatelli (2013), Genard and Cantelli (2008), and Foessel (2010). On the other hand, and Ballet et al. (2014), Déneulin (2014) argue that the differences between them prevail.

DOI: 10.4324/9781003381099-6

Thus, Ricoeur and Sen are halfway between continuity and discontinuity. Regarding the elements of continuity, not only did Ricoeur (2004, 2006) appreciate embeddedness, but also Sen's capability approach. Based on the notion of capabilities, Ricoeur (2004) realized the transition from self-recognition to mutual recognition in one of his final works, *The Course of Recognition*. Conversely, they had two different understandings and roles assigned to the concept of mutuality. Indeed, in his "course of recognition", Ricoeur (2004) ends with the experience of mutual understanding among people for issues related to human rights. Instead, Sen (2004, 2009) probably reached an interest in this research topic in his later works, when Ricoeur had just died.

This chapter is composed as follows: In Section 5.2, we will offer an overview of the key concepts that Ricoeur adopted to compare with Sen's capability approach, in turn, his understanding of economic agents, namely rights and recognition. Subsequently, in Section 5.3, we will highlight how Ricoeur was indebted to Sen, in particular, how his capability approach can be translated into the stage of self-recognition in a philosophical context. In Section 5.4, we will emphasize, instead, what Ricoeur appreciated of Sen's view of economic agents, namely his concept of agency that makes him an alternative voice compared to the early formulation of mainstream *homo oeconomicus* that Ricoeur himself criticized. Then, in Section 5.5, we will discuss the issues for which Ricoeur showed a certain criticism towards Sen, for instance, for his apparently "missing" view of human rights. In Section 5.6, instead, we will highlight how Sen and Ricoeur also differed regarding the relationship between rights and capabilities. Some remarks will conclude this chapter.

5.2 An overview on rights, and recognition in Ricoeur's works

Ricoeur's criticism and debt to Sen are articulated around the concepts of capabilities, rights, and recognition. In particular, the concept of capabilities is what brings Ricoeur closer to Sen, while the concept of rights constitutes the basis for his critique of Sen (Erasmo, 2021). However, we will focus on the influence of Sen's capability approach in Section 5.3, giving priority at this stage to rights and recognition.

To explore Ricoeur's view of rights, it is essential to consider his broader normative framework, which encompasses juridical elements, as well as ethical and moral dimensions. Indeed, Ricoeur explicitly addressed ethical issues in relatively few works: for instance, in *Freedom and Nature* (1966), and more extensively in *Oneself as Another* (1992), where he developed his notion of a "little ethics". In this essay, Ricoeur (1992) re-elaborates earlier ideas on normative concerns such as ethics, freedom, interpretation, narrative, and the self. It is not the case that Cohen and Marsh (2002) considered *Oneself as Another* as a summary of his previous works on action theory, philosophy of action, and narrative theory, but they also explicitly included ethical insights. At the same time, this essay represents Ricoeur's most mature analysis of the human self from an ethical perspective, incorporating hermeneutical, linguistic, and phenomenological elements.

This work centers on three main themes, clearly outlined in its title: (i) a reflexive analysis of the human self; (ii) a dialectical interpretation of the two kinds of identity (idem and ipse) as defined by Ricoeur; and (iii) the dialectic between self and others. The main focus of *Oneself as Another* (1992) is an ethical analysis of the so-called "human capable being", divided between capacities and incapacities. According to Ricoeur (1992), imputability stands at the heart of this analysis – namely the capacity of individuals to recognize themselves as responsible for their actions, primarily through their ability to act, to speak, and to tell. This aspect closely aligns with Sen's capability approach and his effort to reorient economics towards responsibility, through the concept of agency. In this chapter, however, we will concentrate on Ricoeur's "little ethics" because it relates most directly to Sen's understanding of economic agents. For his little ethics, Ricoeur draws on Aristotle and Kant, as they allow movement "from a basic ethic to ethics passing through moral obligation" (Ricoeur, 2007, p. 3). This little ethics is rooted in a Kantian idea of respect, which is guaranteed by rights (Pickett, 2021). In particular, rights give concrete form to the abstract idea of respect between individuals, as originally elaborated by Kant (Seidler, 2009).

In his later works, Ricoeur (2004, 2006) further developed the relationship between ethics and rights. The influence of Hegel on his thinking becomes more pronounced here, especially because Hegel represents what Ricoeur identifies as the missing link between the "is" of Sen's capabilities and the "ought" of rights. In this light, Ricoeur extended his early ethics by integrating Sen's capabilities with Hegel's conception of rights. Accordingly, he argued that the recognition of rights is more significant than other forms of recognition, drawing on Hegel's *Philosophy of Right*, which also emphasized rights that are not formally acknowledged. Unsurprisingly, recognition became one of the leading themes in Ricoeur's later work.

Indeed, *The Course of Recognition*, the book in which Ricoeur most explicitly addresses his debt to and critique of Sen's understanding of economic agents and the capability approach, centers on a redefinition of recognition. Ricoeur (2004) articulates this process in three steps: (i) "recognition as identification", or the stage of identity; (ii) "recognizing oneself", or the stage of alterity where Ricoeur engages with Sen's work; and (iii) "mutual recognition", which represents the apex of a dialectical process between recognition and non-recognition, rooted in Hegel's logic and his idea of rights. This final step also provides a framework for understanding the overall process across the three stages.

5.3 Ricoeur's debt to Sen's capability approach: elaborating the notion of self-recognition

As previously anticipated, Ricoeur (2004, 2006) explicitly mentioned Sen when discussing his intellectual debt regarding the understanding of economic agents and the capability approach in his later works. In "Capabilities and Rights" (2006), which intentionally reverses the title of Sen's "Rights and Capabilities" (1985c), Ricoeur provided a summary of the key issues developed in *The Course of Recognition*. Although this chapter appeared after this book, it is useful to refer to it for introducing the key issues of the *Course*, right for this summary. The main aim of "Capabilities and Rights" is to establish a bridge between capabilities (which, for Ricoeur, belong to the domain of philosophical anthropology) and rights (which belong to the domain of the philosophy of law). In this respect, Ricoeur (2006) argued: "the best candidate for this (…) enterprise is (…) recognition understood as a dynamic process connecting a plurality of points of view as the distinctive steps of the same development" (p. 17).

Recognition is a complex process articulated in three logical steps, as previously introduced: (i) The first step concerns the existentialist dimension of recognition and focuses on "identification", that is, the recognition of the person. (ii) The second step is anthropological and analyses the so-called self-recognition, where Ricoeur discusses the relationship between capabilities (based on Sen's capability approach and his notion of economic agents) and rights. (iii) The third and final step refers to the juridical dimension, where Ricoeur argues in favour of mutual recognition for a juridical acknowledgment of rights, based on Hegel's philosophy of law. This section will focus specifically on the second step, examining: on the one hand, the impact of reflexivity on personal identity in Sen and Ricoeur (§5.2.1); on the other hand, Ricoeur's basic capabilities, including analogies and differences with Sen's capability approach (§5.2.2).

5.3.1 On the impact of reflexivity on personal identity in Sen and Ricoeur

In "Capabilities and Rights", Ricoeur (2006) places the analysis of capabilities squarely within the anthropological dimension of recognition. In particular:

> capabilities belong to the lexicon of human action. It designates the kind of power that we claim to be able to exercise. In its turn this claim expresses the kind of recognition pertaining to the assertion of selfhood at the reflexive level.
>
> (Ricoeur, 2006, p. 17)

Ricoeur (2004, 2006) thus connects capabilities and reflexivity to explain how self-recognition takes place at this stage of the *Course of Recognition*.

He defines capacity as "a kind of power we claim to be able to exercise" (Ricoeur, 2006, p. 17). Crucially, he also clarifies that the verb "claim" refers to a self-assertion, the belief that "I believe that I can" (Ricoeur, 2006). This definition closely resembles Sen's (1980) idea of basic capabilities, which refers to what a person is able to do "certain basic things" (p. 218).

With regard to reflexivity, Ricoeur (2006) sees it as the ability that enables self-recognition and the formation of personal identity. In his earlier work, Ricoeur (1992) distinguishes two forms of identity: *idem* (sameness), which refers to the static and immutable aspect of identity – the ability to "see the self in another" (Pierovich, 2011, p. 69), and *ipse* (selfhood), which refers to the dynamic and evolving aspect of identity over time. Through the dialectic between *ipse* and *idem* – between dynamic and static dimensions – personal identity can be developed and recognized not only from ethical and anthropological perspectives but also from the juridical, political, and social ones.

Interestingly, Sen's notion of commitment shares the same reflexive value as Ricoeur's self-recognition. According to Davis (2007), commitment offers a unified view of the self across three dimensions: self-centred welfare, self-goal choice, and self-welfare goal – as discussed in Chapter 2. This unified perspective supports the development of individual identity (Sen, 1985b), enabling a balance between personal well-being and the well-being of others through the reflexivity embedded in commitment. More specifically, commitment enables individuals to reflect on the aforementioned dimensions – welfare, choices, and goals – shifting them from a private concern to a socially oriented perspective. This social element recalls the influence of Smith's impartial spectator, as noted earlier.

This reconciliation between the individual and social dimensions – achieved through commitment – can be interpreted as an intrapersonal relationship that individuals establish with themselves and their personal identity, mirroring Ricoeur's mechanism of self-recognition. Conversely, when self-interest dominates, individuals fail to exercise reflexivity, and the social dimension of human existence is weakened (Erasmo, 2025). In such cases, others' choices, goals, and well-being are excluded, and social relationships become merely instrumental – oriented towards the maximization of individual well-being.

Considering the impact of economic motives on identity in Sen's framework, it becomes clear that the construction of personal identity is an ongoing process. Giovanola (2009) describes this process as a source of anthropological richness, grounded in the social relationships fostered by commitment as the leading economic motive. Hence, relationality emerges as a key theme in Sen's understanding of economic agents, evoking the Aristotelian view of humans as *zoon politikon*, discussed in Chapter 1.

To conclude this comparison, we can summarize the difference in the sources of reflexivity related to personal identity in Sen and Ricoeur. For Ricoeur, *ipse* is the origin of reflexivity and an intrinsic part of personal identity. For Sen, instead, commitment – an economic motive – serves as the source of reflexivity, shaping personal identity alongside other motivations. Thus, both thinkers reach similar conclusions regarding the importance of reflexivity in building individual identity, although through different processes and starting points.

5.3.2 ***Ricoeur's basic capabilities: analogies and differences with Sen's capability approach***

Following the analysis of reflexivity and identity, we now focus on how Ricoeur understood the relationship between capabilities and self-recognition. Ricoeur (2004) identified a specific set of basic capabilities, also referred to as capacities: the capacity to act, to speak, to tell, and individual imputability. These foundational capabilities culminate in a broader and more specific one – *self-designation.* Ricoeur's basic capabilities clearly show an intellectual debt to Sen's conceptual framework. However, significant differences remain.

For instance, Ricoeur's basic capabilities correspond to what Sen calls functionings. But Ricoeur introduces an important novelty: the distinction between factual and normative capabilities, which is absent in Sen's approach. This distinction captures the transition "from capabilities at large to rights at large" (Ricoeur, 2006, p. 18). In other words, the move is from basic (factual) to specific (normative) capabilities – the former belonging to philosophical anthropology, the latter to the philosophy of law. Methodologically, Ricoeur argues that philosophical anthropology is less specific than philosophy of law, which can offer a more detailed analysis of individual behavior.

Among Ricoeur's basic capabilities, the capacity to speak was already valued in ancient thought, particularly in the works of Aristotle and Homer. Through speech, individuals identify themselves as the "cause" of a given action. This idea persists among contemporary pragmatists, who view speech as the ability to "do things with words" or "being able to say things" (Ricoeur, 2004). But what is the role of this capacity to speak in self-recognition? According to Ricoeur (2004), it enables a gradual process of recognizing oneself and others.

The capacity to act, the second basic capability, refers to the ability to "make events happen" – the power of individuals to influence both their physical and social environments (Ricoeur, 2004, p. 96). By acting, individuals recognize themselves as the "cause of the action" they perform, and their actions generate changes "at the physical, interpersonal, and social level" (Ricoeur, 2006, p. 19).

The third basic capability identified by Ricoeur is the capacity to tell, or the act of telling stories that also refer to the individual self. This ability emerges thanks to the reflexivity that characterizes personal identity, allowing individuals to speak about themselves in narrative terms, thus forming a narrative identity. In this case, we cannot identify any influence of Sen on Ricoeur, since this narrative dimension of personal identity – which also acquires a temporal structure – is absent in Sen's framework.

Instead, the fourth basic capability, which Ricoeur refers to as liability or accountability, is more closely related to Sen's ideas. This accountability "makes the subject accountable before somebody else" and refers to "the ability to bear the consequences of one's own acts, particularly those which are held to be harms inflicted on somebody else as the victim", including "the ability to suffer the pain of punishment" (Ricoeur, 2006, p. 20). This notion of accountability is closely aligned with the sense of responsibility that Sen reintroduced into economics, particularly through the concepts of commitment and agency, discussed, respectively, in Chapters 2 and 4. Imputability plays an additional role in Ricoeur's ethics, as it is the basic capability that makes self-designation possible – a concept that represents the peak of Ricoeur's hierarchical structure of basic capabilities (Ricoeur, 2006).

Thus, self-designation assumes a role comparable to Sen's notion of agency, as it incorporates responsibility into individual behavior. In this direction, referring to Sen's capability approach, Ricoeur (2004) suggested that "capabilities put responsibility in agency". For this reason, capabilities not only represent what an individual or group is able to do or to be in their existence, but they also express individuals' imputability in their actions.

5.4 From Sen's agency and Ricoeur's "rights and capabilities" to their common criticism of mainstream *homo oeconomicus*

In *The Course of Recognition*, Ricoeur turns his attention to Sen's concept of agency and his broader critique of the mainstream *homo oeconomicus*. In doing so, he aligns himself with many of the arguments previously acknowledged in "Capabilities and Rights", including his debt to Sen's articulation of basic capabilities. When Sen (1985d, 1987) developed the idea of agency, he introduced a conceptual distinction that had notable implications for ethical reasoning: the differentiation between agency and well-being. Rather than collapsing the two – as mainstream orthodox economists tend to do – Sen proposed that agency may involve motivations that are not reducible to personal well-being alone. This allows for forms of action driven by commitment, altruism, or public concern.

Ricoeur leverages Sen's agency as a unifying idea for the various expressions of human capacity examined earlier in *The Course*. Through this concept, individual capabilities evolve into social capacities, understood as "claimed by collectivity and submitted to public evaluation and approval" (Ricoeur, 2004, p. 134). In contrast to previous modes of recognition, this shift:

> yields to forms of ethical-juridical justification that bring into play the idea of social justice, as we shall see with the most advanced idea of "capabilities" that I owe to the economist Amartya Sen, which he pairs directly with the idea of rights in the complex expression "rights and capabilities" (or sometimes "rights and agency"). This noteworthy conceptual pair will constitute the most fully developed form of social capacities discussed in this section.
>
> (Ricoeur, 2004, pp. 34–135)

Ricoeur's references to a wide range of authors – from classical sources like Homer and Aristotle to modern thinkers such as Austin, Bergson, Descartes, Kant, and Searle – highlight the depth of his dialogue with Sen. In particular, Sen's work supports Ricoeur's philosophical transition from self-recognition to mutual recognition, or from alterity to reciprocity. Ricoeur's citation points implicitly to two of Sen's significant essays from the 1980s: "Rights and Agency" (1982) and "Rights and Capabilities" (1985c). These works elaborate the relationship between freedom and capabilities, framing them as conditions for meaningful action. Ricoeur uses these arguments to reinforce the idea that rights – grounded in both positive and negative freedom – serve as instruments for expanding individual opportunities and thus for fostering self-recognition.

Although Ricoeur couples rights and agency with rights and capabilities, treating them as interchangeable, in Sen's framework these concepts are related but distinct. While agency involves the capacity to act upon one's values and commitments, capabilities refer to the substantive freedoms that make such actions possible. Agency presupposes responsibility and ethical awareness, while capabilities represent the set of opportunities available to the individual. Thus, agency operates as both a foundation and a condition for the realization of capabilities (Erasmo, 2020). Ricoeur finds this alignment particularly compelling, given its resonance with his own notion of imputability within ethical selfhood.

Ricoeur further emphasizes that social capacities, though diverse, share a common anthropological basis: the power to act, or agency (Ricoeur, 2004, p. 135). He identifies rights and capabilities as the most developed forms of such capacities (Brugiatelli, 2013) and acknowledges:

> I owe the most unexpected, if not the most audacious, of these extensions to the work of Amartya Sen [...]. In his *On Ethics and Economics* (1987), and more precisely in an important work from 1985 titled *Rights and Capabilities*, Sen places the concept of "capabilities" joined with that of "rights" at the centre of his argument in favour of reintroducing ethical considerations into economic theory.
>
> (Ricoeur, 2004, p. 141)

In both *On Ethics and Economics* and "Rights and Capabilities", Sen takes clear steps towards a form of normative economics. This approach likely explains why Ricoeur was drawn to his work. He highlights that Sen, from the outset, seeks to reintegrate moral sentiments into economic behavior (Ricoeur, 2004, p. 142). In doing so, Sen revisits and challenges certain dominant interpretations of Adam Smith's legacy. Specifically, he critiques George Stigler (1971) for misrepresenting Smith's idea of prudence as equivalent to mainstream self-interest, thereby neglecting Smith's broader moral concerns. Sen writes:

> It is instructive to examine how it is that Smith's championing of 'sympathy', in addition to 'prudence' (including 'self-command'), has tended to be so lost in the writings of many economists championing the so-called 'Smithian' view on self-interest and its achievements.
>
> (Sen, 1987, p. 23)

This misreading, common among economists in the 1970s and 1980s, led to an overemphasis on *The Wealth of Nations*, while largely ignoring Smith's earlier ethical work. As a result, Smith was wrongly cast as a precursor to *homo oeconomicus* (Polanyi, 1944). As Ricoeur notes, many economists of that era were:

> almost unanimous in considering economic actors in terms of their motives, where such motivation has been reduced to its rational core, itself interpreted as the maximizing of self-interest, in accordance with the principle of utility.
>
> (Ricoeur, 2004, p. 142)

Ricoeur highlights how Sen's work (1977, 1985b) took a sharply different path. Sen (1987) argues:

> We can see the person, in terms of agency, recognizing and respecting his or her ability to form goals, commitments, values, etc., and we can also see the person in terms of well-being, which too calls for attention. This dichotomy is lost in a model of exclusively self-interested motivation, in which a person's agency must be entirely geared to his own well-being. But once that straitjacket of self-interested motivation is removed, it becomes possible to give recognition to the indisputable fact that a person's agency can well be geared to considerations not covered—or at least not fully covered—by his or her own well-being.
>
> (p. 41)

Ricoeur appreciates Sen's refusal of a monistic view of person in economics. By distinguishing agency from well-being, Sen recovers a richer moral anthropology that echoes Ricoeur's own ethical framework. While Ricoeur had already developed a parallel understanding through the concept of imputability (1992), he recognizes in Sen a complementary voice. This shared concern ultimately fuels Ricoeur's broader critique of *homo oeconomicus*, which he sees as "a simplified image of this model of what motivates a person to act" (Ricoeur, 2004, p. 142).

5.5 How Ricoeur distanced himself from Sen: the relevance of mutual recognition and human rights

In the final section of "Capabilities and Rights", Ricoeur distances himself from Sen by favouring Hegel's conception of rights. This shift, however, appears to stem from a partial reading of Sen's work: If rights and capabilities can only be linked within a juridical context, it suggests that Ricoeur may not have engaged with Sen's later contributions. Notably, he does not reference Sen's theory of human rights, developed in the early 2000s. It is likely that Ricoeur was only familiar with Sen's earlier writings from the 1980s (Erasmo, 2019b). For example, *Elements of a Theory of Human Rights* (2004), where Sen explicitly addresses juridical issues, came out shortly before Ricoeur's death in 2005 – perhaps too late to be considered in his final works.

In concluding "Capabilities and Rights", Ricoeur marks the passage from self-recognition to mutual recognition through a linguistic shift: from active to passive verbs, that is, from "the claim to recognize" to "the need to be recognized" (Ricoeur, 2006, p. 21). This introduces the dimension of mutuality – absent in both self-recognition and, according to Ricoeur, in Sen's thought. In fact, Ricoeur suggests that only within the juridical domain can rights and capabilities be meaningfully connected. Despite "empruntant à l'économiste Amartya Sen le concept de 'capabilité'", Ricoeur recognizes instead a "droit à acquérir des capacités" (Foessel, 2010, p. 123), ultimately rejecting Sen's framework due to its lack of reciprocity, which he saw as essential for reconciling rights and capabilities.

Although Sen never explicitly discusses reciprocity, his work contributed significantly to the emergence of relational goods – a point that makes the distinction with Ricoeur somewhat more nuanced than it might initially appear (Erasmo, 2019a).

In Sen's goal rights system (1982), rights to certain capabilities have an ethical rather than a juridical value. Unlike Ricoeur, Sen does not ground rights in formal legal systems. Hegel, by contrast, focuses on "universality linked to the conquest of new rights at the level of juridical relationship at large", where the legal person is "the bearer of rights implying normative obligations as regards the other partner in this kind of relationship" (Ricoeur, 2006, p. 24). For Ricoeur, rights and capabilities can converge in this universal juridical space – a convergence he finds lacking in Sen's account.

With the transition to mutual recognition, Ricoeur sees an opportunity to enrich basic capabilities through the conjunction between the universal validity of the norm and the singularity of the persons (Ricoeur, 2006, p. 24). This opens the door to new and more robust capabilities, enabled by the juridical recognition of rights. This extension of the normative sphere simultaneously generates "the enumeration of new subjective rights" and "the ascription of these rights to new categories of individuals or of groups" (Ricoeur, 2006, p. 24). These new rights include civil rights (such as those concerning life, mobility, and property), political rights (like participation in public life), and social rights (such as equitable access to basic goods). In the concluding section of his analysis, Ricoeur even moves beyond the juridical dimension, reaching what he calls *social esteem*, an idea reminiscent of Habermas (Busacchi, 2015). This could be considered a fourth stage in the recognition process – focused on the acknowledgment of social status or rank. However, this level presents complications, as the diverse social mediations involved require different forms of esteem depending on one's social role (see also Boltanski and Thévenot, 1991).

While Ricoeur denies the presence of a juridical or universal dimension in Sen's work, Sen had in fact developed a detailed theory of *human rights*, emphasizing both their ethical foundation and public legitimacy. Notably, in *Elements of a Theory of Human Rights* (2004), the word *recognition* appears 21 times, and an entire section is devoted to *Recognition, Agitation and Legislation.* Sen defines human rights as "primarily demands. They are not principally 'legal', 'proto-legal' or 'ideal-legal' commands". Although these rights often inspire laws, this is "a further fact, rather than a constitutive characteristic of human rights" (Sen, 2004, p. 319). He further argues:

> The implementation of human rights can go well beyond legislation, and a theory of human rights cannot be sensibly confined within the juridical model in which it is frequently incarcerated. For example, public recognition and agitation can be part of the obligations—often imperfect—generated by the acknowledgement of human rights.
>
> (Sen, 2004, pp. 319–320)

Thus, for Sen (2004), human rights are grounded in ethical claims that can survive open and informed scrutiny – an "interactive process of critical scrutiny" (pp. 320–321). This highlights two essential aspects: mutuality and universality. In Sen's view, the latter depends on the former. Mutuality unfolds in public reasoning – reproducing in society the same reflexive process that commitment enables at the individual level (as discussed in Section 5.3). In Section VII of *Elements of a Theory of Human Rights*, Sen observes that most literature focuses on the legislation and institutionalization of human rights. However, he argues that:

> Legislation is an important domain of public action," but "there are other ways and means which are also important and often effective in advancing the cause of recognized human rights.
>
> (Sen, 2004, p. 343)

Among the three routes identified – recognition, active agitation, and legislation – Sen gives special emphasis to the first two. Recognition, as he explains, must be "distinguished from the legislative route", as it simply involves acknowledging certain claims as fundamental human rights, without requiring legal enforcement. This sharply contrasts with Ricoeur's view, where recognition and legislation are inseparable.

Sen instead emphasizes the ethical force of human rights: their recognition can lead to social acknowledgment and legitimacy, even without coercive enforcement. This social recognition aligns closely with Ricoeur's fourth stage of recognition – social esteem – though Sen arrives there through a different, non-juridical path. The second route, active agitation, refers to organized efforts to defend and promote rights – such as public advocacy or monitoring violations. These actions may target rights with or without legal status but are crucial in Sen's framework. Unlike recognition, agitation involves enforcement mechanisms (though not necessarily legal ones), creating social pressure for change. The third route, legislation, is the most institutionally formalized – and the most prominent in contemporary history. Yet Sen (2004) expresses caution: He argues that legal enforcement is not always necessary, stating: "If a human right is important, then it must be ideal to legislate it into a precisely specified legal right" (p. 345). Still, he maintains that advocacy and public reasoning are often more effective and preferable to coercive legislation – highlighting a fundamental divergence from Ricoeur's position.

5.6 Exploring rights and capabilities: "rights to certain capabilities" and the "capacity for choice about life" as evaluative criteria in Sen's theory of justice

Ricoeur also diverged from Sen in how he envisioned a concrete way to move beyond the early model of *homo oeconomicus* typical of mainstream economics. In his view, the real alternative lay in reclaiming freedom and rights, which should be translated into actual opportunities for individuals. This line of thought is directly tied to his critique of what he perceived as an insufficiently developed theory of human rights in Sen's work. For Ricoeur, overcoming the *homo oeconomicus* means reinterpreting freedom and rights as components that make individual choice genuinely possible. Drawing on Sen's normative economics, Ricoeur (2004) sought to relate individual freedoms both to life choices and to collective responsibility, extending this connection into the realm of political and legal evaluation. This synthesis is grounded in the dual notions of positive and negative freedom, as outlined by Sen (1982). Negative freedom is aligned with civil rights, and its maximalist interpretation reflects libertarian thinking; positive freedom, by contrast, encompasses what a person is effectively able to do or become, building upon negative freedom but going further – towards the genuine capacity to choose one's life path.

As Ricoeur affirmed:

> The rights that political economy must incorporate into the motives for economic action are components of the idea of 'capabilities', as he argues in his *Rights and Agency*.[1] The most worthy expression in this regard is that of 'rights to certain capabilities'.
>
> (Ricoeur, 2004, p. 143)

This idea corresponds to Sen's goal-rights framework. Ricoeur saw in it an alternative to the dominant ethical models of the time, stating that such a framework allows us to: "Go beyond the alternative between consequentialism, stemming from the theory of well-being (such as utilitarianism), and a deontological approach, founded on constraints external to agency" (Ricoeur, 2004, p. 143).

For Ricoeur, "rights to certain capabilities" provide a foundation for Sen's theory of justice, in which exercising rights expands individual freedoms. This marks a shift in Ricoeur's own thinking – from viewing capabilities as anthropological features to recognizing the need to identify and protect these capabilities through political and legal means. He then examined his reflection, contrasting Sen's evaluative approach with the utilitarian tradition, which judges outcomes by achieved utility. Instead, Ricoeur emphasized: "It is in terms of the liberty to accomplish things, as an extension of positive liberty, that Sen bases social evaluation—for example, of competing policies. Thereby, individual liberty understood as a life choice becomes a social responsibility" (Ricoeur, 2004, p. 145).

According to Ballet and Mahieu (2009), however, this notion of social responsibility remains limited in Sen's framework, as it is grounded solely in individual freedoms and does not necessarily entail individual responsibility. Thus, it becomes a critical and possibly weak point in Sen's view of economic agents. Ricoeur (2004) nonetheless insisted that:

> The conceptual revolution introduced with the pair 'rights' and 'capabilities' will be understood only if we contrast it with the evaluation of action in terms of utility and well-being. It is a real capacity for choice about life that this capability is promoted to the rank of a criterion for evaluating social justice.
>
> (p. 146)

This shift marks a fundamental departure from welfarism and from Rawls's (1971) theory of justice. It is made possible by Sen's introduction of alternative rational economic motives and the dualistic conception of the person in ethical calculation, as discussed earlier. Ricoeur identifies this key criterion – "capacity for choice about life" – as the central element in Sen's framework for assessing justice across political systems.

However, this same criterion, while powerful in political and economic analysis, becomes a point of divergence between the two thinkers. According to Ricoeur, its abstraction and lack of institutional grounding hinder the possibility of mutual recognition. Ultimately, this limitation explains why Ricoeur concluded his engagement with Sen's thought and turned instead towards Hegel's concept of *Anerkennung*, which offers a juridical and institutional model of recognition. Like Hegel (1807 [1977]) and later Honneth (1992), Ricoeur aimed to institutionalize recognition, something he felt was absent in Sen's ethics of freedom.

5.7 Concluding remarks

In this chapter, we offer a view on the intellectual relationship between Paul Ricoeur and Amartya Sen, not only by identifying their shared concerns – such as the centrality of capabilities and ethical responsibility – but also by clarifying their divergences, especially regarding the conditions for mutual recognition and the juridical grounding of rights. While Ricoeur explicitly draws on Sen's capability approach – especially in his shift from self-recognition to mutual recognition – he ultimately distances himself from Sen's position by insisting on the necessity of institutionalized recognition and juridical universality for rights and capabilities to be meaningfully reconciled. This criticism highlights potential weaknesses in Sen's view of economic agents.

Sen, by contrast, remains cautious about grounding rights in legal or mutual recognition frameworks, preferring instead to emphasize the role of agency because it is among the leading characteristics of his view of economic agents. In turn, his notion of rights as "demands" that survive public scrutiny marks a significant departure from Ricoeur's Hegelian model of recognition. However, this precise difference helps sharpen the distinctive features of Sen's normative economics and the anthropological assumptions underpinning it.

From this perspective, the comparison with Ricoeur is not just a philosophical exercise; it becomes an essential tool for better understanding Sen's conception of economic agents. In his view, individuals are not utility-maximizing individuals defined by self-interest, as in early formulations of *homo oeconomicus*, nor are they fully embedded in juridically reciprocal structures, as in Ricoeur. Rather, Sen's agents are capable beings (from a capability perspective), shaped by agency, responsibility, and commitment. We can conclude that, among the limits of Sen's understanding of economic thought has probably controversial institutional foundations, given the role he assigned to rights. At the same time, Ricoeur probably did not read Sen's works on human rights, as well as his masterpiece *An Idea of Justice* (2009), in which he offered a more complex view of the institutional framework. However, this missing reading of Sen's most recent works is not a limit for us, because we are privileged to Sen's early view of economic agents.

Note

1 There is a relevant issue with one of the most authoritative English translations of the *Parcours de la Reconnaissance*, by David Pellauer, the same adopted in this book. In this respect, Pellauer failed to refer to the right Sen's work quoted by Ricoeur in his original French version, confusing "Rights and Agency" with *Commodities and Capabilities* (1985a). This is why I substitute his translation with Sen's work mentioned by Ricoeur in the original French version of his book, "Rights and Agency".

References

Ballet, J., Bazin, D., Dubois, J.-L. and Regis, M. F. (2014). *Freedom, Responsibility and Economics of the Persons*, New York: Routledge.

Ballet, J. and Mahieu, F. R. (2009). "Capabilité et Capacité dans le Développement: repenser la question du Sujet dans l'oeuvre d'Amartya Sen", *Revue Tiers Monde*, 198 (2), 303–316.

Boltanski, L. and Thévenot, L. (1991). *De la Justification. Les Ėconomies de la Grandeur*, Paris: Ėditions Gallimard.

Brugiatelli, V. (2013). "Paul Ricoeur e Amartya Sen su Facoltà di Agire e Giustizia Sociale", *Archivio di Filosofia*, 8–1(1–2): 117–127.

Busacchi, V. (2015). "Habermas and Ricoeur on Recognition: Toward a New Social Humanism", *International Journal of Humanities and Social Sciences*, 5 (2), 10–20. http://hdl.handle.net/11584/98154

Cohen, R. A. and Marsh, J. L. (2002). *Ricoeur as Another: The Ethics of Subjectivity*, State University of New York.

Davis, J. B. (2007). Identity and Commitment: Sen's Fourth Aspect of the Self. In P. Fabienne and H. B. Schmid (eds.), *Rationality and Commitment*, Oxford: Oxford University Press, pp. 313–335.

Déneulin, S. (2014). *Well-Being, Justice and Development Ethics*, London: Routledge.

Erasmo, V. (2019a). Beni relazionali e impresa editoriale, *Rivista di Società Italiana di Filosofia Politica*, 1–19.

Erasmo, V. (2019b). "The Foundational Decade to Amartya Sen's Capability Approach (1970–1980)", *Rivista di Storia Economica*, 35 (3), 295–326. https://doi.org/10.1410/98221

Erasmo, V. (2020). Homo Capabilitiensis. Un paradigma antropologico per il futuro ispirato alla riflessione di Amartya Sen. In L. Alici and F. Miano (eds.), *L'Etica nel Futuro*, Salerno: Orthotes, pp. 455–464.

Erasmo, V. (2021). "Mutual Recognition: the missing link from the "is" of capabilities to the "ought" of rights. An analysis of Amartya Sen and Paul Ricoeur's "dialogue"." *Critical Hermeneutics*, 5 (2), 247–276.

Erasmo, V. (2025). "Extending the Capabilities Conception of the Individual in Economics: Relationality and Responsibility", *Journal of Interdisciplinary Economics*, 37 (1), 25–41.

Foessel, M. (2010). "Du Sujet économique à l'homme capable", *Revue des Deux Mondes*, 116–127.

Genard, J. L. and Cantelli, F. (2008). "Êtres Capable et Compétents: Lecture anthropologique et Pistes Pragmatiques. Being Capable and Skilled: Anthropological Reading and Pragmatic", *SociologieS*, 1–23. https://doi.org/10.4000/sociologies.1943

Giovanola, B. (2009). *Etica ed Economia: il rapporto possibile*, Padova: Editore Messaggero.

Hegel, F. (1977). *Phenomenology of Spirit*, Oxford: Oxford University Press.

Honneth, A. (1992). *Kampf um Anerkennung, Grammatik sozialer Konflikte*, Frankfurt am Main: Suhrkamp.

Pickett, H. (2021). Doing Time and Narrative: Teaching in (and Out of) Prisons With Paul Ricoeur. In D. Boscaljon and J. F. Keuss (eds.), *Paul Ricoeur and the Hope of Higher Education*, London: Lexington Books, pp. 277–302.

Pierovich, A. (2011). *Understanding Paul Ricoeur's "Oneself as Another"*, Ariadne Press.

Polanyi, K. (1944). *The Great Transformation*, New York City: Farrar and Rinehart.

Rawls, J. (1971). *A Theory of Justice: Revised Edition*, Harvard: Harvard University Press (1999). https://doi.org/10.2307/j.ctvkjb25m

Ricoeur, P. (1966). *Freedom and Nature: The Voluntary and the Involuntary*, Northwestern University Press.

Ricoeur, P. (1992). *Oneself as Another*, Chicago: The Chicago University.

Ricoeur, P. (2004). *The Course of Recognition*, Trans. by David Pellauer, Cambridge: Harvard University Press.

Ricoeur, P. (2006). Capabilities and Rights. In S. Déneulin, M. Nebel and N. Sagovsky (eds.), *Transforming Unjust Structures. The Capability Approach*, Berlin: Springer, pp. 17–26.

Ricoeur, P. (2007). *Reflections on the Just*, Chicago: University of Chicago Press.

Seidler, V. (2009). *Kant, Respect and Injustice (Routledge Revivals): The Limits of Liberal Moral Theory*, New York: Routledge.

Sen, A. (1977). "Rational Fools: A Critique of the Behavioural Foundations of Economic Theory", *Philosophy &Public Affairs*, 6 (4), 317–344.

Sen, A. (1980). *Equality of What?* The Tanner Lecture on Human Values, Cambridge: Cambridge University Press, 195–220.

Sen, A. (1982). "Rights and Agency", *Philosophy and Public Affairs*, 11 (1), 3–39.

Sen, A. (1985a). *Commodities and Capabilities*, Amsterdam: North Holland.

Sen, A. (1985b). "Goals, Commitment and Identity", *Journal of Law, Economics& Organization*, 1 (2), 341–355.

Sen, A. (1985c). Rights and Capabilities. In T. Honderich (ed.), *Morality and Objectivity*, London: Routledge, pp. 130–148.

Sen, A. (1985d). "Well-Being, Agency and Freedom. The Dewey Lectures, 1984", *The Journal of Philosophy*, 82, 169–221.

Sen, A. (1987). *On Ethics and Economics*, Oxford: Basil Blackwell.

Sen, A. (2004). "Elements of a Theory of Human Rights", *Philosophy and Public Affairs*, 32 (4), 315–356.

Sen, A. (2009). *The Idea of Justice*, Cambridge: Harvard University Press.

Stigler, G. J. (1971). "Smith's Travel on the Ship of the State", *History of Political Economy*, 3 (2), 265–277.

6 Reading social enterprises (SEs) through Sen's view of economic agents

Commitment, social embeddedness, and self-sacrifice

6.1 Introduction

Building on the distinguishing features of Sen's understanding of economic agents, we use these concepts to analyse social enterprises (SEs), which are among the firms that most explicitly privilege sociality in their activities. In this regard, Sen has not directly engaged with business organizations. This makes the perspective offered here more original. On the one hand, this chapter contributes to the theoretical debate on the complex nature of SEs by adopting Sen's perspective on economic agents, primarily highlighting commitment, self-sacrifice, and social embeddedness; on the other hand, it illustrates both the potentialities (particularly the role of commitment in promoting social goals) and the weaknesses (notably the risk of self-sacrifice) of SEs that stem from their social embeddedness, while also discussing measures aimed at mitigating these limits.

In this respect, Sen's understanding of economic agents offers three interrelated dimensions that are particularly relevant for analysing SEs: the role of commitment as an economic motive, the social embeddedness of SEs, and the possibility of self-sacrifice arising from an extremization of commitment. SEs occupy a distinctive position within the broader context of business organizations because they pursue social goals while remaining profit-oriented, thus functioning as hybrid enterprises that combine these two dimensions (Battilana et al., 2012; Billis, 2010). Traditional analyses have often contrasted SEs with neoliberal businesses, presenting them as opposing models. However, this interpretation is limiting, as SEs also incorporate profit within their mission. Through the lens of Sen's framework, we offer new insights into this comparison by showing how agency and economic motives further illuminate the complexity of SEs. In particular, we suggest that a useful way to distinguish, without juxtaposing, SEs and neoliberal businesses is to consider that the former exhibit a higher degree of social embeddedness than the latter.

By integrating these elements, this chapter also bridges normative and empirical perspectives on SEs, highlighting the interplay between economic

DOI: 10.4324/9781003381099-7

motives, institutional design, and social context. Moreover, it extends Sen's understanding of economic agents beyond abstract theorization, demonstrating its explanatory power in interpreting real-world organizational dynamics, including both the opportunities and the constraints that arise in the pursuit of social impact (for instance, when self-sacrifice becomes extreme). In doing so, this chapter positions SEs not only as hybrid organizations but also as spaces where the ethical, social, and economic dimensions of human agency converge.

This chapter is structured as follows. Sections 6.2 and 6.3 trace the historical roots of SEs within the civil economy tradition and the early social economy, including definitional debates around SEs. Subsequently, Sections 6.4 and 6.5 analyse SEs through Sen's notion of commitment and his broader understanding of economic agents, emphasizing agency, responsibility, and social embeddedness as analytical tools for approaching SEs from a different perspective. Finally, Section 6.6 examines the possibility of self-sacrifice within SEs, providing concrete examples from the literature and, in turn, suggesting possible measures – drawing on Sen's understanding of economic agents – to counterbalance this economic motive and mitigate its negative impact on individuals' well-being.

6.2 The historical roots of SEs: the civil economy tradition

Before exploring SEs through some of the distinguishing features of Sen's conception of economic agents, we first outline their historical roots within the tradition of the civil economy. This perspective enables us to return to thinkers already discussed in Chapter 1, such as Aristotle, Thomas Aquinas, and Antonio Genovesi, whose contributions extend well beyond early reflections on economic motives in philosophy and theology (Alford, 2026; Bruni, 2013; Santori, 2020). Indeed, they can be regarded as among the earliest contributors to the broader and enduring tradition of the civil economy (Bruni et al., 2021).

The civil economy emerged at a peculiar moment in European history. During the eighteenth century, the continent was shaped by a large-scale anti-feudal movement and by a providential understanding of commerce and the market (Bruni, 2018). Among the leading exponents of this political and economic perspective were Italian scholars such as Antonio Genovesi and Giacinto Dragonetti who became central figures in the Neapolitan Catholic Enlightenment (Bruni and Porta, 2003). For more than two centuries, the European society had long been dominated by rural and consumption-oriented virtues. Thus, the civil approach emerged as a response rooted in the Catholic and humanistic spirit of Europe, to counter the mentioned-above "vicious" trend. This background helps explain why the civil economy tradition has, since its origins, been deeply rooted in Catholic principles and values (Santori, 2022; Zamagni, 2010).

In this context, the civil economy tradition developed rapidly and soon gained international recognition. It is not by chance that the first academic chair in Economics in the world was established in Naples in 1753 as a chair of civil economy, with Antonio Genovesi as its first holder (Zamagni, 2021). The concept of civil economy was also used by Neapolitan scholars to refer to "public happiness" (Porta, 2016). One of Genovesi's most famous maxims states that "[i]t is a universal law that we cannot make ourselves happy without making others happy as well" (Genovesi, 1962, p. 449). According to Genovesi (1783), civil economy is always oriented towards happiness, which has a fundamentally social nature, as already discussed in relation to Aristotle in Chapter 1. It is not sufficient to live in well-being to be happy, since happiness can grow further when others are also both happy and prosperous. Thus, the Neapolitan civil economy tradition is rooted not only in Catholic principles and values but also in the Aristotelian tradition (Bruni, 2014).

Based on these Catholic origins, the civil economy tradition suggests that economic agents should be oriented towards collective growth, understood as the common good (in Latin *bonum comune*), in line with Aristotelian ethics. However, these roots provided more than an understanding of collective growth because they also contributed, in turn, to shaping a new perspective on economics. Written between the thirteenth and fifteenth centuries, the works of Antonino da Firenze, Bernardino da Siena, Nicola d'Oresme, and Thomas Aquinas offered key insights into economic matters – money, theories of just price, fair wages, and usury, finance (Januard, 2025) – alongside a vision of society in which the good arises from virtues rather than self-interest (Bruni, 2018). Among these scholars, Aquinas stands out as the most authoritative voice shaping an economic perspective that would later inspire the development of the civil economy tradition.

In this respect, Aquinas directly influenced Genovesi's works and contributed to what Santori (2021) defined as the "Mediterranean spirit of capitalism", as already noted. Both Aquinas and Genovesi shared the Aristotelian view that economic agents are "social animals", naturally oriented towards promoting the welfare of others (Santori, 2021), as discussed in Chapter 1. According to Aquinas, political friendship represents the common good of society, binding its members together in peace and prosperity. In this sense, political friendship is closely linked to human flourishing and the practice of virtues (Santori, 2020). The civil economy tradition inherited this optimistic view of sociality as a natural human disposition that fosters collective happiness through friendship and cooperation. At the same time, consistent with its Catholic origins, it acknowledges that the effects of "original sin" also wound human nature. Nevertheless, economic agents retain the capacity to act virtuously and promote societal happiness through their innate sociality (Erasmo, 2022).

In this respect, both Aquinas and Genovesi grounded their analysis of economic agents in the concept of reciprocity as a relational virtue. This notion is foundational to what Genovesi later defined as mutual assistance in market dynamics aimed at promoting collective well-being, or the common good (Hodge, 2025; Nalli, 2023). Thus, reciprocity becomes the distinguishing feature of the Mediterranean spirit of capitalism, with implications in both economic and political domains. On the one hand, it promotes mutual concern in market dynamics, since mutual assistance can coexist with self-interested behavior in market exchanges (Bruni, 2008; Sacchetti and Sugden, 2009); on the other hand, it implies that institutions play a central role in fostering collective well-being (Pabst, 2018). For Genovesi, mutual assistance embodies all the civil virtues that can promote collective well-being. Furthermore, mutuality implies that every party involved in a market transaction is willing to promote the interests of others alongside their own. Indeed, the fundamental law of the market is mutual benefit (Bruni and Santori, 2022); in turn, the market does not exist in isolation from other social spaces where economic agents live their relationships, whether as individuals or firms. It follows that every market transaction establishes a social relationship.

Over time, the concept of mutuality has evolved significantly across different fields. In this respect, contemporary scholarship has further developed Aquinas and Genovesi's ideas. According to these recent exponents of civil economy (Bruni et al., 2008; Gui, 2021; Nalli and Santori, 2023; Sugden, 2018; Zamagni, 2007, among others), markets can be designed to promote mutual benefit, while SEs identify those firms that actively generate mutual benefit in market transactions (Blasi and Michie, 2025; Borzaga and Sforzi, 2014). This contemporary revival of the civil economy approach seeks to reintroduce ethics into economics, countering the value-free view of economic discipline, typical of mainstream neoclassical orthodox economics (Robbins, 1932).

By tracing the civil economy from its medieval roots through the Italian Enlightenment, the contemporary civil economy tradition highlights how markets can once again become spaces for reciprocity and civil virtues, ultimately contributing to the promotion of the common good and collective well-being. Particular emphasis is placed on reciprocity as an intrinsic feature of economic agents, stemming from their social nature. Based on the role assigned to social relationships in economic life, we might say that this tradition adopts an embedded conception of economic agents. In particular, it views the market as a space for mutual benefit. This is possible because the civil economy tradition has always interpreted market transactions as social relationships, grounded in values such as relationality and responsibility. However, the mainstream neoclassical paradigm became dominant with the marginalist revolution, and its hegemony persists today, along with a tendency towards social atomism in the understanding of economic agents.

This explains why some contemporary civil economy research groups and movements are actively seeking to renew the economic framework or develop new economic models. Among them, the international movement "Economy of Francesco", inspired by Franciscan values and Pope Francis's pontificate (Rotondi and Santori, 2023), and the community "Renaissance in Economics", which advocates for new economic paradigms based on a manifesto that includes civic engagement of academic scholars among its five pillars (for more, see Becchetti et al., 2024), stand out.

After this overview of the civil economy tradition, we can argue that SEs can be fruitfully examined through the lens of Amartya Sen, revealing a potentially mutually reinforcing relationship between their respective theoretical bases. In particular, Sen can provide SEs – originating within the civil economy tradition, which emphasizes civic and social dimensions – with a rigorous framework for analysing economic motives, bridging the sociality inherent in the civil economy with the formal analytical tools of mainstream economics, without adopting social atomism. At the same time, the civil economy tradition underpinning SEs could be seen as a potential extension of Sen's thought, addressing the lack of mutuality highlighted by Ricoeur, as discussed in Chapter 5. In this book, however, we focus exclusively on the first aspect, namely the application of Sen's framework to SEs, leaving the exploration of the second point for future research.

In the next section, we examine the origins of SEs, which emerged within this tradition, highlighting how these organizations embody the principles of mutuality, civic responsibility, and the vision of economic agents as inherently social and embedded in their communities.

6.3 SEs within the social economy: historical evolution and definitional debates[1]

SEs situate within the broader spectrum of the social economy. In this respect, the social economy encompasses a wide array of organizational forms, united by a commitment to social objectives, civic responsibility, and the promotion of collective well-being. Understanding this diversity helps to contextualize SEs as part of a broader set of socially oriented economic activities, rather than as isolated phenomena. In particular, the spectrum of the social economy includes a variety of organizational forms, for instance: (i) entrepreneurial associations and foundations, which often emerge to address social needs unmet by the state or private markets, combining philanthropic goals with structured organizational practices (Borzaga and Defourny, 2004; Defourny and Nyssens, 2010). These entities typically rely on voluntary participation while also developing managerial capacities to ensure sustainability. (ii) Traditional cooperatives and mutual aid societies, organized around principles of self-help, collective ownership, and democratic governance (Gui, 1991).

These organizations provide goods, services, or employment opportunities to their members, while promoting social solidarity and equitable economic participation. (iii) Social cooperatives, which represent a more recent and explicitly social-oriented evolution of the cooperative model, particularly prevalent in Italy since the 1970s. These cooperatives often integrate disadvantaged or marginalized individuals into the labor market, offering social services such as healthcare, education, and community support. They are mission-driven, blending social objectives with entrepreneurial strategies to ensure economic viability and long-term impact. The common thread of these organization forms is the integration of social goals with economic activity, a principle aligned with the broader civil economy tradition already analysed in the previous section. Within this spectrum, SEs occupy a unique position because they combine market engagement with a direct "commitment" (not so different from Sen's understanding of the concept) to social goals, operationalizing values such as reciprocity, civic responsibility, and social embeddedness. All these elements confirm the relevance of SEs for this book.

The historical origins of SEs can be traced to the Italian Catholic tradition and to widespread civic engagement and community-oriented economic practices in the pre-war period (Ianes, 2016), which contributed to the early development of the social economy, including SEs and cooperatives. Across various countries, local initiatives and associations emerged to address social needs neglected by the state or private markets, often guided by ethical, religious, or civic motivations. These early forms of collective action laid the foundations for what later became known as the social economy, encompassing a diverse set of organizations committed to social objectives alongside economic activity.

Between the 1960s and 1970s, many activists inspired by civic and religious values began promoting new bottom-up initiatives aimed at defending the rights of more vulnerable social groups and creating services in response to the profound transformations affecting the Italian economy during those years (Testi et al., 2017). Until the end of the 1970s, the non-profit sector attracted limited attention from European scholars, with the exception of some political scientists and sociologists who focused on voluntary or civil organizations and their impact on public social policies (Borzaga et al., 2014). By contrast, economists mainly concentrated on cooperatives as non-profit firms during the same period.

The crisis of European welfare systems at the beginning of the 1970s created the conditions for extending the debate on SEs beyond Italian borders. This crisis can be analysed from various perspectives, but the most relevant here is Hansmann's analysis (1979). According to him, economic agents are selfish and opportunistic in their decision-making. From a neo-institutionalist perspective, he also argued that market failures in the provision of welfare services arise due to information asymmetry regarding quality and contractual incompleteness (Borzaga and Sacconi, 2022). These failures created space for private initiatives, which were increasingly required to meet the demand for social services. Borzaga et al. (2014) observed that non-profit initiatives developed after the 1970s appeared more autonomous and entrepreneurial than traditional non-profit organizations. Thus, SEs began to evolve in form while maintaining their commitment to collective well-being, especially for the most vulnerable members of society. It is no coincidence that the term "social enterprise" was introduced by the EMergence des Entreprises Sociales en Europe (EMES) European Research Network during those years (Defourny and Nyssens, 2014).

Although they had an important goal and became very common in Italy, SEs initially did not benefit from support from public authorities. Since the 1980s, however, SEs have also been increasingly considered in Europe because of the crisis of the welfare state. In 1991, these new organizations were finally institutionalized as 'social cooperatives' and began to be funded by public resources to promote their social activities, especially from a locally based perspective (Birkhölzer, 2009). Thanks to these funds, cooperatives have the necessary financial resources to promote the diffusion and growth of SEs, enhance the quality of their services, and collaborate with local governments. All these activities are oriented towards enhancing the community's sense of well-being, as well as promoting social integration and human development throughout the society. This orientation to general interest is where civil economy and SEs converge, as they share common interests in improving collective well-being from a social perspective.

So, this analysis of the origins and development of SEs shows how these organizations are the outcome of a non-linear evolutionary process, deeply embedded in the tradition of the civil economy, in voluntary action, in cooperative practices, and in civic responses to welfare transformations. The hybridization of profit and social objectives, entrepreneurial activity, and participatory governance has gradually distinguished SEs within the broader social economy, giving rise to a wide variety of organizational forms.

Alongside this complex and articulated historical trajectory, however, it is not equally straightforward to identify a single, unambiguous definition of SEs. This should not be seen as a weakness, but rather as a reflection of their richness: SEs operate across a broad spectrum of organizational arrangements, confirming their plural and open nature, as well as their capacity to adapt to the evolving needs of society.

According to the early definitions of SEs, these organizations might be described through three main criteria (Borzaga and Defourny, 2004), namely (i) the economic and entrepreneurial dimension of SEs (a continuous activity producing goods and/or providing services, a significant level of economic risk, and a minimum amount of paid work); (ii) the social dimension of SEs (an explicit aim to benefit the community, an initiative launched by a group of citizens or civil society organizations, and limited profit distribution); (iii) the participatory governance of SEs (a high degree of autonomy, decision-making power not based on capital ownership, and a participatory structure involving various parties affected by the activity).

However, this definition does not exhaust the complexity of the phenomenon. Over the last two decades, several definitions of SEs have emerged, each emphasizing different dimensions of their multifaceted nature. This reflects the high degree of pluralism in the debate around SEs. Among the most well-known definitions, Young and Lacy (2014) use the metaphor of a zoo to capture this diversity, suggesting that SEs comprise multiple "species", each with distinct features while sharing the common essence of being "social" enterprises. Other scholars adopt a more "minimalist" approach, equating SEs with social entrepreneurship: "A social entrepreneur will simply be someone who organizes and/or operates a venture or corporation, which features social goals" (Peredo and McLean, 2006, p. 57).

Although this definition does not specify what these "social goals" entail and tends to conflate the entrepreneur with the enterprise, thereby overlooking organizational complexity, it rightly emphasizes the role of individuals (or groups of individuals) as foundational for the existence of SEs. However, this explanation is only partial (Aisaiti et al., 2021; Ebrahim et al., 2014; Ometto et al., 2019). The growing relevance of corporate social responsibility (CSR) initiatives within neoliberal firms further complicates the boundaries between these two types of organizations, making them a bit ambiguous (Brandsen and Karré, 2011; D'Aunno et al., 1991; Romanelli, 1991; Tracey et al., 2011).

In this context, however, the concept of hybridity (Doherty et al., 2014) provides a useful analytical lens. Since at least the 1980s, indeed, scholars have described SEs as hybrid organizations (Battilana et al., 2012; Billis, 2010). In particular, Battilana and Lee (2014) define SEs as entities that integrate "both business and charity at their cores" (p. 397), addressing a unique trade-off between their social and economic activities, so as to generate enough revenues without losing sight of their social purpose (Ebrahim et al., 2014, p. 82). Similarly, Drancheva and Au (2021) argue that SEs may embody the "family institutional logic", even when not family-owned, by "caring about specific social issues or people" and fostering "caring relationships among members of the organization" (p. 78). These features help delineate the distinctive nature of SEs.

The hybrid nature of SEs can give rise to what appears to be a paradox because they integrate social objectives with the need to ensure financial sustainability (Child, 2019). For instance, Ebrahim et al. (2014) note that balancing these two dimensions may create challenges for SEs' long-term viability. Child (2019), however, suggests that the perceived paradox becomes less rigid when the comparison with neoliberal firms is considered more carefully. Although neoliberal enterprises may display forms of social engagement through CSR initiatives, their core orientation remains linked to profit maximization. In many cases, CSR functions primarily as a response to consumer expectations for ethically produced goods. This alone is, therefore, insufficient to explain what differentiates SEs from neoliberal enterprises.

In other words, the literature on SEs highlights the coexistence of multiple, and occasionally contrasting, motivations shaping their missions, structures, and operational logics. This plurality complicates attempts to converge on a single, universally accepted definition of SEs, unlike the neoclassical tradition, which offers a clearer conceptual formulation of the "firm" (e.g., Johnson, 1972; Shapiro and Shapiro, 1976).

The following analysis seeks to reconcile these apparently conflicting motives within the broader framework of Amartya Sen's view of economic agents (Erasmo and Migheli, 2026). Specifically, it argues that the economic behavior and motives adopted by SEs can be coherently interpreted through Sen's (1977, 1985a, 1985b) notions of commitment and self-sacrifice, previously discussed in Chapters 2 and 3, as well as through social embeddedness (Davis, 2024).

In this way, following the methodological call to challenge the assumptions underpinning dominant business theories (Alvesson and Sandberg, 2011), the analysis offers an alternative perspective. By showing how SEs' social imprinting enhances social performance through embeddedness, while potentially constraining economic productivity through commitment and (sometimes) self-sacrifice, this reading of SEs through Sen's understanding of economic agents provides a new theoretical foundation for explaining their hybrid nature, contributing to a pluralistic and open definitional debate within the business organization and social economy literature.

6.4 Sen's notion of commitment as the leading motive of SEs

Sen's concept of commitment offers a valuable lens to better understand the hybrid nature of SEs. According to Sen (1977), as already discussed in Chapter 2, commitment refers to the motivation that drives individuals to act based on ethical and social principles, extending beyond the traditional assumption of self-interested economic agents whose utility functions ignore social concerns.

As Sen (1982, pp. 7–8) stressed, "'commitment' is concerned with breaking the tight link between individual welfare (with or without sympathy) and the choice of action". Subsequently, Sen (1985b) pointed out that commitment can lead individuals not only to make decisions that diminish their own welfare but also to depart from purely self-interested motives. According to this view of economic agents, social norms act as a guiding force, enabling individuals to transcend self-interest in pursuit of other-regarding goals. This perspective allows us to move beyond the neoclassical model of *homo oeconomicus*, supporting the pursuit of collective and social objectives (Anderson, 2000), also when we refer to firms, not just individuals in economics.

Based on their hybrid nature which also incorporates social goals, commitment implies proactive actions by SEs to counter socioeconomic injustice. For this reason, SEs sometimes willingly accept lower profits than their neoliberal counterparts, prioritizing human development and social equity over mere financial gain. Their choices reflect a dedication to reducing social and economic inequalities in society. In particular, commitment is essential both at the level of entrepreneurs and employees to maintain a delicate balance between social goals and financial profitability (Erasmo and Migheli, 2026). Alongside this ideal balance, SEs focus on the enhancement of social capabilities (Migheli, 2011), precisely because their economic actions are driven by commitment to improving others' well-being. The focus on social capabilities also suggests that SEs carry a deeper sense of social responsibility compared to neoliberal businesses, as commitment intrinsically entails ethical accountability in economic decision-making. This responsibility represents a moral engagement central to SEs' operational philosophy that makes them different from neoliberal firms.

In this respect, these latter often engage in CSR initiatives, which could give the impression that they are socially embedded actors because their projects often aim to address social problems, including environmental degradation or the support of marginalized populations. While these initiatives can yield positive societal outcomes, the main goal for neoliberal firms remains profit maximization (Friedman, 1970; Palladino, 2022). So, CSR functions as a strategy to maintain consumer loyalty among socially conscious buyers, rather than as an intrinsic social mission. Consequently, CSR alone does not transform neoliberal firms into SEs, because, for SEs, social objectives are central to the mission.

To highlight how these theoretical principles are applied in practice, the following examples demonstrate how SEs operationalize commitment and prioritize social goals while navigating economic activity, in turn, showing a "higher degree of social embeddedness" compared to other firms. For instance, Grameen Bank in Bangladesh prioritizes microloans to empower women and reduce poverty, often accepting modest financial returns in favor of fostering social development (Yunus et al., 2010). Similarly, "The Big Issue", a SE in the UK, provides employment opportunities for marginalized individuals, reflecting a commitment to social inclusion that exceeds profit considerations (Teasdale, 2010). Another example is Arizmendi Bakery in the United States, a worker-owned cooperative that integrates democratic decision-making and profit-sharing, demonstrating how economic activity can be embedded in collective social responsibility (Marraffino, 2009).

These realities exemplify Sen's commitment as the leading economic motive, willingly taking actions that prioritize societal welfare and human development over narrow financial optimization, in line with Sen's framework.

Through such examples, it becomes evident that SEs operationalize commitment by embedding social considerations into core strategic and operational decisions. By doing so, they demonstrate how the pursuit of social capabilities and ethical objectives can coexist in a firm that places social purpose at the centre of economic life.

6.5 Agency, responsibility, and social embeddedness: distinguishing features of Sen's view of economic agents to read SEs

Further elements to read SEs through the lens of Sen's understanding of economic agents are the notions of agency, responsibility, and social embeddedness. As discussed in Chapter 4, agency refers to the capacity of individuals to pursue goals they have reason to value, extending beyond individual well-being to include ethical and social considerations (Sen, 1987). This dualistic conception of the person in ethical calculus, distinguishing but connecting agency and well-being, provides the foundation for interpreting economic action not merely as the pursuit of self-interest but also as an exercise of moral responsibility (Sen, 1985a, 1987).

In practice, SEs embody this duality in an organizational context: Their economic activity contributes to well-being both for the organization and for the communities they serve, while agency ensures that such activities are guided by socially oriented objectives. Thus, SEs can be understood as expressions of collective agency (Scarlato, 2013), enabling individual actions that contribute to broader social development. This perspective highlights the hybrid nature of SEs, where economic rationality and ethical engagement coexist. In this respect, agency in SEs can be examined at both individual and collective levels, where entrepreneurs and employees act as agents who form commitments and values that guide organizational goals, taking into account others' objectives and adjusting their own choices accordingly (Crocker, 2008; Erasmo, 2022).

In this regard, the relationship between agency and responsibility in SEs reflects Sen's view of an embedded impartial spectator (Chapter 2), who is not morally neutral but exercises reasoned judgment shaped by ethical and social principles (Sen, 1977, 1982, 1985b). In SEs, this translates into strategic decisions that balance financial sustainability and social goals. In particular, entrepreneurs exemplify responsible agency by fostering human development and equity, often at the cost of immediate profit, consistent with Sen's understanding of rationality as encompassing more than material payoffs. Although SEs and neoliberal firms share some practices, such as engagement with social issues, the underlying motivations may differ. In this regard, neoliberal firms may adopt CSR initiatives, but these initiatives often serve instrumental purposes, such as enhancing reputation or responding to consumer expectations, rather than expressing an intrinsic social mission (Friedman, 1970; Palladino, 2022). By contrast, SEs reflect a more explicit ethical engagement, which can be understood through Sen's concept of agency. When agents act responsibly, they consider how their decisions affect others, extending individual accountability into collective domains (Migheli, 2011). In this way, ethical considerations are embedded within organizational processes and the social relationships that constitute these networks, enabling economic actions to be coordinated towards the enhancement of social capabilities (Sferrazzo and Ruffini, 2021; Weaver, 2019). Thus, responsibility becomes both a guiding principle and an operational reality, as SEs make deliberate choices that balance financial performance with social outcomes, reflecting an ongoing commitment to ethical and social objectives.

About Sen's idea of agency, individuals can rationally act in ways that might reduce their own well-being if such actions advance broader societal benefits (Alkire, 2005). The same applies for actions made by SEs. In this sense, commitment enables SEs to integrate responsibility into decision-making, ensuring that financial sustainability does not overshadow social aims. In Sen's works, the ethical dimension of responsibility is reinforced by the dualistic conception of the person, as agents navigate between personal achievements and socially oriented goals (Sen, 1987). This "dualistic conception of the firm" is evident in SEs, where responsibility is not peripheral but central to strategic and operational choices.

The component that connects agency and responsibility within SEs is, again, social embeddedness. As noted, social embeddedness refers to the extent to which economic agents are situated within social relationships and networks that shape their behavior and decisions (Archer, 1995; Granovetter, 2007). In SEs, embeddedness enhances agency by providing the relational context through which commitment and responsibility are enacted because entrepreneurs and employees are not isolated: Their decisions emerge within networks of interactions, shared norms, and mutual obligations. In this way, embeddedness reinforces collective responsibility by creating structures in which ethical and social considerations are sustained across organizational levels. The relationships fostered by SEs enable individuals to coordinate actions towards socially desirable outcomes, thus operationalizing commitment as a rational economic motive. In this context, social embeddedness also strengthens the development of social capabilities (Migheli, 2011): through networks of mutual accountability and shared norms, SEs support collective actions that expand opportunities for disadvantaged groups and promote social cohesion. The relational dimension of economic action, therefore, complements the ethical and rational aspects of agency, creating a framework in which social, moral, and economic considerations are addressed simultaneously.

Integrating Sen's concepts of agency, responsibility, and social embeddedness offers a useful theoretical lens for understanding the distinctive nature of SEs, not as the opposite of neoliberal businesses, but as organizations where economic and ethical logics interact more tightly. SEs embody what we might define through the formula of "dualistic conception of the firm", where agency (as an ethical foundation for economic decisions and social relationships) and well-being (or profits) virtuously coexist. In particular, agency enables entrepreneurs and employees to act with purpose and ethical awareness, while responsibility ensures that decisions reflect consideration of others' goals and well-being.

Finally, social embeddedness situates these actions within networks that sustain ethical behavior and collective outcomes. Together, these elements illustrate how SEs operationalize commitment in practice, balancing economic rationality with social and ethical objectives. SEs thus exemplify hybrid organizations where moral engagement, social responsibility, and economic activity coexist, demonstrating the relevance of Sen's framework for understanding economic agents, not only individuals but also firms.

6.6 Self-sacrifice as one of the limits of SEs: some examples from social economy literature

Certainly, SEs are not without limitations. Drawing on Sen's understanding of economic agents, one of the potential weaknesses that may emerge within SEs is about the notion of self-sacrifice, discussed in Chapter 5. Sen's conception of self-sacrifice helps illuminate how, within organizations that prioritize social goals over profit, the motivational structure of agents may shift from commitment, a rational stance that incorporates ethical considerations and the well-being of others, towards behavior that can unintentionally undermine the organization's economic viability. When the sense of social responsibility becomes excessive or misinterpreted, commitment may morph into self-sacrifice, leading individuals to make decisions that significantly reduce profits or diminish their own well-being. This vulnerability does not concern only employees, but also entrepreneurs who may equally fall prey to perception biases that frame economically suboptimal decisions as morally required, in turn, reinforcing self-sacrifice as the prevailing economic motive in SE dynamics.

In this respect, empirical literature on the social economy is useful to offer several examples that help illustrate how this dynamic manifests in practice. A possible case to be considered is that of healthcare cooperatives in Italy, particularly in regions such as Lombardy and Emilia-Romagna (Villotti et al., 2014). Many of these cooperatives provide home-care services for elderly and vulnerable patients. In these realities, it is not uncommon for nurses and social workers to take on overtime hours or additional tasks (Erasmo, 2020), for instance, for accompanying patients to medical appointments or responding to emergencies outside contractual schedules. These practices undeniably support community well-being and ensure the continuity of care activities. At the same time, they also create conditions of chronic stress and increase the risk of burnout among caregivers. In this regard, empirical studies show that this form of self-sacrifice tends to be more pronounced among women, aligning with Folbre's (2004) theoretical insights on the gendered nature of care work and the risk of altruistic exploitation.

A similar pattern can be observed within educational SEs. For example, Italian organizations such as "Maestri di Strada" in Naples or the "Giovanni Paolo II Foundation" in Milan involve teachers, educators, and volunteers in sustained tutoring, mentoring, and extracurricular activities directed towards students from marginalized backgrounds. Equally, international programs (including "Teach for America" in the United States or "Room to Read" in Asia and Africa) operate according to comparable logics. In this respect, although these initiatives often succeed in improving educational outcomes and supporting vulnerable youth, they demand significant emotional and temporal investment from educators (Gicheva, 2022), which may result in professional stagnation or personal strain. Here again, the social mission may outweigh individual well-being, illustrating that commitment can evolve into self-sacrifice, affecting both employees and organizational sustainability.

Other examples within SEs that might be expressed through Sen's notion of self-sacrifice as an extremization of commitment are fair-trade and ethical production cooperatives. In Italy, organizations like "Libera Terra" or "Alce Nero" rely on workers engaged in labor-intensive agricultural and food-processing activities, often characterized by seasonality and physical effort (Travasi and Mutignani, 2023). A strong sense of mission, combined with commitment to environmental and social sustainability, frequently motivates workers to assume demanding tasks without receiving compensation proportional to their effort. On the international stage, cooperatives such as "Divine Chocolate" in Ghana or "Hand in Hand" in India display similar characteristics, especially where women's labor is central and personal dedication systematically surpasses formal contractual obligations (ILO, 2024). These cases demonstrate how within mission-oriented work environments, self-sacrifice often becomes structural, a normalized component of labor dynamics.

Social care and community-based enterprises provide additional evidence of this tendency at a local and global perspective. In Italy, cooperatives such as "Il Millepiedi" in Tuscany assign educators and care workers responsibilities that extend far beyond basic assistance, including the organization of recreational activities, training programs, and family support services. International organizations (for instance, "Special Olympics" or "Sense International") often depend on volunteers who routinely exceed the expectations attached to their formal roles. These mission-driven forms of engagement mirror Sen's idea of self-sacrifice as an action motivated by moral considerations even when such actions negatively affect individual well-being.

Despite their socially desirable aims, these examples illustrate how SEs may embody internal dynamics that reveal the ambivalent side of commitment when it transforms into self-sacrifice. This analysis reinforces the need to read SEs through the nuanced lens offered by Sen's understanding of economic agents and economic motives, which highlights both the ethical strengths and the potential vulnerabilities inherent in organizations grounded in social responsibility and collective values.

6.7 Concluding remarks

After an overview of the civil economy tradition and the origins and development of SEs, we joined the definitional debate about SEs, emphasizing how their hybrid nature might also be expressed through the distinguishing features of Sen's understanding of economic agents. In this respect, Sen's emphasis on the plurality of economic motives (including commitment and self-sacrifice) has been useful in highlighting how SEs can harness the commitment of workers to achieve social goals. At the same time, economic motives might contribute to structural and institutional vulnerabilities that may lead to excessive self-sacrifice among the people involved in SEs, in turn, worsening their individual well-being. Through the analysis of some concrete examples, we show that SEs frequently rely on a complete dedication of their workforce to maintain social impact, where the sense of commitment might easily shift into self-sacrifice. At the same time, these cases from social economy reveal how misaligned recognition systems, uneven workload distribution, and limited professional development opportunities can constrain individual agency, potentially undermining long-term social sustainability.

This joint reading of Sen's understanding of economic agents and SEs adds new elements to the open debate around these complex business organizations. In particular, it highlights the importance of considering workers not merely as inputs to organizational performance, but as agents whose capabilities and agency shape the effectiveness and sustainability of social impact. In turn, applying the distinguishing features of Sen's understanding of economic agents to SEs, it emerges that self-sacrifice might be an extremization of commitment, thus leading to a conclusion that goes beyond Sen's works. This aspect will be further explored in the general conclusions of this work.

Note

1 Sections 6.3, 6.4, and 6.5 are partially indebted to another work coauthored with Migheli (2026).

References

Aisaiti, G., Liang, L., Liu, L., Xie, J. and Zhang, T. (2021). "How Social Enterprises Gain Cognitive Legitimacy in the Post-Pandemic Period? Social Welfare Logic and Digital Transformation", *Industrial Management and Data Systems*, 121 (12), 2697–2721.

Alford, H. (2026). "The Influence of Thomistic Thought in Contemporary Business Ethics". In Luetge, C. & Ziegler M. T. (eds.), *Handbook of the Philosophical Foundations of Business Ethics*, Dordrecht: Springer Netherlands, pp. 1–27.

Alkire, S. (2005). "Subjective Quantitative Studies of Human Agency", *Social Indicators Research*, 74 (1), 217–260. https://doi.org/10.1007/s11205-005-6525-0

Alvesson, M. and Sandberg, J. (2011). "Generating Research Questions Through Problematization", *Academy of Management Review*, 36 (2), 247–271. https://doi.org/10.5465/amr.2009.0188

Archer, M. S. (1995). *Realist Social Theory: The Morphogenetic Approach*, Cambridge: Cambridge University Press.

Battilana, J. and Lee, M. (2014). "Advancing Research on Hybrid Organizing–Insights from the Study of Social Enterprises", *Academy of Management Annals*, 8 (1), 397–441. https://doi.org/10.5465/19416520.2014.893615

Battilana, J., Lee, M., Walker, J. and Dorsey, C. (2012). "In Search of the Hybrid Ideal", *Stanford Social Innovation Review*, 10 (3), 51–55.

Becchetti, L., Biggeri, M., Biondo, A. E., Corsi, M., Cucculelli, M., De Castris, M., … and Venturini, A. (2024). "Making Sense of the Five Critical Pillars: A Manifesto for Economics Renaissance", SSRN 4916063.

Billis, D. (2010). "Towards a Theory of Hybrid Organizations". In D. Billis (ed.), *Hybrid Organizations and the Third Sector*, Basingstoke: Palgrave Macmillan, pp. 46–69.

Blasi, J. and Michie, J. (2025). "Realising the Mutual Advantage", *International Review of Applied Economics*, 39 (4–5), 485–491. https://doi.org/10.1080/02692171.2025.2528484

Borzaga, C., Bodini, R., Carini, C., Depedri, S., Galera, G. and Salvatori, G. (2014). "Europe in Transition: The Role of Social Cooperatives and Social Enterprises", Europe in Transition: The Role of Social Cooperatives and Social Enterprises by Carlo Borzaga, Riccardo Bodini, Chiara Carini, Sara Depedri, Giulia Galera, Gianluca Salvatori: SSRN.

Borzaga, C. and Defourny, J. (2004). *The Emergence of Social Enterprise*, Psychology Press.

Borzaga, C. and Sacconi, L. (2022). "Discorsi sull'Impresa Sociale. Un Confronto Tra Carlo Borzaga e Lorenzo Sacconi", *Impresa Sociale*, 4, 4–25.

Borzaga, C. and Sforzi, J. (2014). "Social Capital, Cooperatives and Social Enterprises". In Christoforou, A. and Davis, J. B. (eds.), *Social Capital and Economics*, Routledge, pp. 193–214. https://doi.org/10.4324/9780203505014

Brandsen, T. and Karré, P. M. (2011). "Hybrid Organizations: No Cause for Concern", *International Journal of Public Administration*, 34, 827–836. https://doi.org/10.1080/01900692.2011.605090

Bruni, L. (2008). *Reciprocity, Altruism and Civil Society: In Praise of Heterogeneity*, Abingdon, Oxon: Routledge.

Bruni, L. (2013). "On Virtues and Awards: Giacinto Dragonetti and the Tradition of Economia Civile in Enlightenment Italy", *Journal of the History of Economic Thought*, 35(4), 517–535. https://doi.org/10.1017/S105383721300031X

Bruni, L. (2014). "Commerce, Reciprocity, and Civil Virtues: The Contribution of the Civil Economy". In *Commerce and Community*, Routledge, pp. 85–100.

Bruni, L. (2018). "Capitalism and Its New-Old Religion: A Civil Economy Perspective", *Journal for Markets and Ethics*, 6 (1), 121–131.

Bruni, L., Gilli, M. and Pelligra, V. (2008). "Reciprocity: Theory and Facts: Introduction to the Special Issue", *International Review of Economics*, 55 (1), 1–11. https://doi.org/10.1007/s12232-008-0042-9

Bruni, L. and Porta, P. L. (2003). "Economia civile and Pubblica Felicità in the Italian Enlightenment", *History of Political Economy*, 35(5), 361–385.

Bruni, L. and Santori, P. (2022). "The Illusion of Merit and the Demons of Economic Meritocracy: Which Are the Legitimate Expectations of the Market?, *Journal of Business Ethics*, 176 (3). https://doi.org/10.1007/s10551-020-04727-7

Bruni, L., Santori, P. and Zamagni, S. (2021). *Lezioni di Storia del Pensiero Economico: Un Percorso dall'Antichità al Novecento*, Roma: Città Nuova.

Child, C. (2019). "Whence Paradox? Framing Away the Potential Challenges of Doing Well by Doing Good in Social Enterprise Organizations", *Organization Studies*, 41 (8), 1147–1167. https://doi.org/10.1177/0170840619857467

Crocker, D. A. (2008). *Ethics of Global Development: Agency, Capability, and Deliberative Democracy*, Cambridge: Cambridge University Press.

D'Aunno, T., Sutton, R. I. and Price, R. (1991). "Isomorphism and External Support in Conflicting Institutional Environments: A Study of Drug Abuse Treatment Centers", *Academy of Management Journal*, 34, 636–661.

Defourny, J. and Nyssens, M. (2010). "Conceptions of Social Enterprise and Social Entrepreneurship in Europe and the United States: Convergences and Divergences", *Journal of Social Entrepreneurship*, 1 (1), 32–53. https://doi.org/10.1080/19420670903442053

Defourny, J. and Nyssens, M. (2014). "The EMES Approach of Social Enterprise in a Comparative Perspective". In Defourny, J., Hulgard, L. and Pestoff, V. (eds.), *Social Enterprise and the Third Sector*, London: Routledge, pp. 42–65.

Doherty, B., Haugh, H. and Lyon, F. (2014). "Social Enterprises as Hybrid Organizations: A Review and Research Agenda", *International Journal of Management Reviews*, 16, 417–436. https://doi.org/10.1111/ijmr.12028

Ebrahim, A., Battilana, J. and Mair, J. (2014). "The Governance of Social Enterprises: Mission Drift and Accountability Challenges in Hybrid Organizations", *Research in Organizational Behavior*, 34, 81–100. https://doi.org/10.1016/j.riob.2014.09.001

Erasmo, V. (2020). "Oltre le Specificità di Genere. Cura e Diritti nella Prospettiva Relazionale di Amartya Sen e Martha Nussbaum", *SocietàMutamentoPolitica*, 11(22), 151–161.

Erasmo, V. (2022). "Paolo Santori, Thomas Aquinas and the Civil Economy Tradition: The Mediterranean Spirit of Capitalism (London: Routledge, 2021), pp. 174", *Journal of the History of Economic Thought*, 44 (4), 667–670.

Erasmo, V. and Migheli, M. (2026). "Reading Social Enterprises (SEs) Through Sen's Notion of Commitment", *Journal of Economic Interaction and Coordination*, 1–20.

Folbre, N. (2004). "A Theory of the Misallocation". In Folbre, N. & Bittman, M. (eds.), *Family Time: The Social Organization of Care*, London: Routledge, pp. 7–24.

Friedman, M. (1970). "The Social Responsibility of Business is to Increase its Profits". *The New York Times Magazine*. https://www.nytimes.com/1970/09/13/archives/a-friedman-doctrine-the-social-responsibility-of-business-is-to.html

Genovesi, A. (1783). *Lezioni di commercio o sia d'economia civile*, vol. I, Napoli: Stamperia Simoniana.

Genovesi, A. (1962). *Autobiografia e Lettere*, Milano: Feltrinelli.

Gicheva, D. (2022). "Altruism and Burnout: Long Hours in the Teaching Profession", *ILR Review*, 75 (2), 427–457. https://doi.org/10.1177/0019793920981055

Granovetter, M. (2007). "Economic Embeddedness [1985]", *Contemporary Sociological Theory*, 2 (3), 162.

Gui, B. (1991). "The Economic Rationale for the "Third Sector", *Annals of Public and Cooperative Economics*, 62 (4), 551–572.

Gui, B. (2021). "In Search of a Market Morality for Making Real the 'Community of Advantage': A Note on Sugden's 'Principle of Mutual Benefit'", *International Review of Economics*, 68 (1), 131–140. https://doi.org/10.1007/s12232-021-00365-1

Hansmann, H. B. (1979). "The Role of Nonprofit Enterprise", *Yale Law Journal*, 89, 835.

Hodge, C. (2025). "Fraternity as Mutual Aid or Mutual Assistance? From Political Fraternity to Economics of Francesco", *International Review of Economics*, 72 (2), 25. https://doi.org/10.1007/s12232-025-00497-8

Ianes, A. (2016). "Exploring the Origins of Social Enterprise: Social Co-Operation in the Italian Welfare System and its Reproduction in Europe (from the 1970s to the present), Euricse Working Paper n°88/16, Exploring the Origins of Social Enterprise: Social Co-operation in the Italian Welfare System and Its Reproduction in Europe (From the 1970s to the Present) by Alberto Ianes: : SSRN

International Labour Organization. (2024). *Strengthening Women's Cooperatives: The SEWA Model and Beyond*. ILO. https://www.ilo.org/sites/default/files/2024-11/ILO-SEWA%20report_final_web%20version.pdf

Januard, P. (2025). "Thomas Aquinas on Production and Financing", *The European Journal of the History of Economic Thought*, 1–37. https://doi.org/10.1080/09672567.2025.2530398

Johnson, G. L. (1972). "Alternatives to the Neoclassical Theory of the Firm (NTE)", *American Journal of Agricultural Economics*, 54 (2), 295–303. https://doi.org/10.2307/1238716

Marraffino, J. (2009). "The Replication of Arizmendi Bakery: A Model of the Democratic Worker Cooperative Movement. *Grassroots Economic Organizing (GEO) Newsletter*, 2 (3).

Nalli, F. and Santori, P. (2023). "The Economic Principle of Political Liberalism: A Comparison of Rawls and Sugden", *Review of Political Economy*, 35 (2), 476–493. https://doi.org/10.1080/09538259.2021.1951476

Nalli, F. (2023). "What Mutual Assistance Is, and What It Could Be in the Contemporary World", *Journal of Business Ethics*, 182 (4), 1041–1053. https://doi.org/10.1007/s10551-021-04936-8

Ometto, M. P., Gegenhuber, T., Winter, J. and Greenwood, R. (2019). "From Balancing Missions to Mission Drift: The Role of the Institutional Context, Spaces, and Compartmentalization in the Scaling of Social Enterprises", *Business & Society*, 58 (5), 1003–1046. https://doi.org/10.1177/0007650318758329

Palladino, L. (2022). "Economic Policies for Innovative Enterprises: Implementing Multi-Stakeholder Corporate Governance", *Review of Radical Political Economics*, 54 (1), 5–25. https://doi.org/10.1177/04866134211026691

Peredo, A. M. and McLean, M. (2006). "Social Entrepreneurship: A Critical Review of the Concept", *Journal of World Business*, 41, 56–65. https://doi.org/10.1016/j.jwb.2005.10.007

Porta, P. L. (2016). "The Idea of Happiness in Italy". In Bruni, L & Porta, P. L. (eds.), *Handbook of Research Methods and Applications in Happiness and Quality of Life*, Cheltenham: Edward Elgar Publishing, pp. 499–520.

Robbins, L. (1932). *An Essay on the Nature and Significance of Economic Science*, London: Macmillan.

Romanelli, E. (1991). "The Evolution of New Organizational Forms", *Annual Review of Sociology*, 17, 79–103. https://doi.org/10.1146/annurev.so.17.080191.000455

Rotondi, V. and Santori, P. (2023). *Rethinking Economics Starting from the Commons*, Switzerland: Springer.

Sacchetti, S. and Sugden, R. (2009). "The Organization of Production and Its Publics: Mental Proximity, Market and Hierarchies", *Review of Social Economy*, 67 (3), 289–311. https://doi.org/10.1080/00346760802621906

Santori, P. (2020). "Donum, Exchange and Common Good in Aquinas: The Dawn of Civil Economy", *The European Journal of the History of Economic Thought*, 27 (2), 276–297. https://doi.org/10.1080/09672567.2020.1720764

Santori, P. (2021). *Thomas Aquinas and the Civil Economy Tradition: The Mediterranean Spirit of Capitalism*, London: Routledge.

Santori, P. (2022). "Is Relationality Always Other-Oriented? Adam Smith, Catholic Social Teaching, and Civil Economy", *Philosophy of Management*, 21 (1), 49–68. https://doi.org/10.1007/s40926-021-00175-z

Scarlato, M. (2013). "Social Enterprise, Capabilities and Development Paradigms: Lessons from Ecuador", *Journal of Development Studies*, 49 (9), 1270–1283. https://doi.org/10.1080/00220388.2013.790962

Sen, A. (1977). "Rational Fools: A Critique of the Behavioural Foundations of Economic Theory", *Philosophy & Public Affairs*, 6 (4), 317–344.

Sen, A. (1982). "Rights and Agency", *Philosophy and Public Affairs*, 11 (1), 3–39. https://www.jstor.org/stable/2265041

Sen, A. (1985a). *Commodities and Capabilities*, Amsterdam: North Holland.

Sen, A. (1985b). "Goals, Commitment and Identity", *Journal of Law, Economics & Organization*, 1 (2), 341–355. https://doi.org/10.1093/oxfordjournals.jleo.a036895

Sen, A. (1987). *On Ethics and Economics*, Oxford: Basil Blackwell.

Sferrazzo, R. and Ruffini, R. (2021). "Are Liberated Companies a Concrete Application of Sen's Capability Approach?, *Journal of Business Ethics*, 170, 329–342. https://doi.org/10.1007/s10551-019-04324-3

Shapiro, N. and Shapiro, N. (1976). "The Neoclassical Theory of the Firm", *Review of Radical Political Economics*, 8 (4), 17–29. https://doi.org/10.1177/048661347600800403

Stout, L. A. (2008). "Why We Should Stop Teaching Dodge v. Ford", *Virginia Law and Business Review*, 3 (1), 164–176.

Sugden, R. (2018). *The Community of Advantage: A Behavioural Economist's Defence of the Market*, Oxford: Oxford University Press.

Teasdale, S. (2010). "Models of Social Enterprise in the Homelessness Field", *Social Enterprise Journal*, 6 (1), 23–34. https://doi.org/10.1108/17508611011043039

Testi, E., Bellucci, M., Franchi, S. and Biggeri, M. (2017). "Italian Social Enterprises at the Crossroads: Their Role in the Evolution of the Welfare State", *Voluntas: International Journal of Voluntary and Nonprofit Organizations*, 28 (6), 2403–2422. https://doi.org/10.1007/s11266-017-9875-8

Tracey, P., Phillips, N. and Jarvis, O. (2011). "Bridging Institutional Entrepreneurship and the Creation of New Organizational Forms: A Multilevel Model", *Organization Science*, 22, 60–80. https://doi.org/10.1287/orsc.1090.0522

Travasi, A. and Mutignani, F. (2023). "Rural Entrepreneurship and the Craving for Organic Food: Two Interrelated Market Dimensions. Evidence from a Single Case Study", *International Journal of Economic Behavior*, 13 (1), 133–148. https://doi.org/10.14276/2285-0430.4272

Villotti, P., Zaniboni, S. and Fraccaroli, F. (2014). "Social Cooperatives in Italy", *L'Encéphale*, 40, S57–S65. https://doi.org/10.1016/j.encep.2014.04.002

Weaver, R. L. (2019). "Social Enterprise and the Capability Approach: Exploring How Social Enterprises Are Humanizing Business", *Journal of Nonprofit & Public Sector Marketing*, 32 (5), 427–452. https://doi.org/10.1080/10495142.2019.1589630

Yunus, M., Moingeon, B. and Lehmann-Ortega, L. (2010). "Building Social Business Models: Lessons from the Grameen Experience", *Long Range Planning*, 43 (2–3), 308–325. https://doi.org/10.1016/j.lrp.2009.12.005

Zamagni, S. (2007). *L'Economia del Bene Comune*, Roma: Città Nuova.

Zamagni, S. (2010). "Catholic Social Thought, Civil Economy, and the Spirit of Capitalism". In Finn, D. K. (ed.), *The True Wealth of Nations: Catholic Social Thought and Economic Life*, Oxford: Oxford University Press, pp. 63–93.

Zamagni, S. (2021). *Prosperità Inclusiva: Saggi di Economia Civile*, Studium Edizioni.

Concluding remarks

In this book, we have achieved three main results. First, Sen's view of economic agents provides a systematic alternative to *homo oeconomicus*, highlighting the roles of commitment and self-sacrifice in what we defined here as Sen's embedded impartial spectator. Second, agency emerges as the conceptual foundation for a dualistic conception of the person, in which responsibility and well-being, ethical reflection, and practical action co-exist. Third, social enterprises (SEs) exemplify that organizations, like individuals, can integrate economic profits and social goals, translating Sen's economic agents and economic motives into operational and socially meaningful practices.

For this purpose, this analysis highlights a trajectory from historical reflections on economic behavior to contemporary organizational applications, stressing the conceptual richness and practical relevance of Sen's view of economic agents and economic motives, often neglected in favour of other dimensions of his thought (among others, the capability approach or his idea of human development). In this respect, one of the most relevant achievements of this book is to demonstrate that Sen's view of economic agents and economic motives offers a strong alternative to early formulations of *homo oeconomicus*, an issue that remains highly relevant for contemporary economics, especially the social one. Whereas mainstream *homo oeconomicus* emphasizes atomistic self-interest as the leading motive of economic action, Sen understands economic agents as socially embedded. In this context, social embeddedness arises from two additional economic motives: commitment and self-sacrifice.

In particular, commitment represents a positive force in economic behavior, enabling agents to integrate ethical concerns and the goals and choices of others into their decision-making. In this sense, commitment restores the social dimension in economics by acknowledging that individual decisions are rarely isolated. Self-sacrifice, instead, appears as a form of "extremization" of commitment. When economic agents are overly focused on others' well-being, they risk neglecting their own. While self-sacrifice illuminates important dynamics of moral motivation, it carries a more ambivalent value than commitment, reflecting the tension between ethical engagement and the

DOI: 10.4324/9781003381099-8

sustainability of individual well-being. These two economic motives, therefore, provide a nuanced, context-sensitive alternative to the narrowly self-interested model of *homo oeconomicus*, revealing the plurality of motives that shape economic behavior.

The common ground for commitment and self-sacrifice is the concept of agency, which underpins a dualistic conception of the person. More specifically, agency explains how individuals can act responsibly, taking into account the interests of others, while simultaneously achieving their own well-being. This duality situates ethical reflection and practical action within a single framework, bridging individual and collective dimensions of economic life. In this respect, agency enables economic agents to navigate trade-offs, pursue morally informed goals, and exercise their capabilities in ways that enhance both individual and social well-being. Sen's embedded impartial spectator provides a lens through which agents can evaluate the consequences of their choices in a socially and morally informed manner. On the one hand, self-sacrifice may render economic agents highly socially embedded, but it may also reduce their impartiality. On the other hand, commitment fosters a balance between social embeddedness and impartiality in economic behavior and ethical judgments related to economic life.

Subsequently, we have argued that these general characteristics that Sen attributes to economic agents, often explicitly referring to individuals, can also be extended to business organizations. In particular, agency, commitment, self-sacrifice, and social embeddedness are consistent with the definition of SEs. Indeed, SEs integrate social and financial objectives, balancing ethical engagement with economic sustainability. In this sense, SEs exemplify what we defined here as the "dualistic conception of the firm". Similarly to individuals, these organizations pursue social goals while attending to the well-being of both internal stakeholders and external communities. This parallel underscores the relevance of Sen's framework for interpreting organizational dynamics in hybrid and mission-driven settings. In this way, SEs have become a laboratory for exploring the normative and operational implications of Sen's view of economic agents, showing how commitment can drive social impact, how agency enables responsible decision-making, and how social embeddedness facilitates coordination towards social goals. At the same time, SEs are also useful for reflecting on some potential limits related to Sen's understanding of economic agents. An overextension of commitment may lead to forms of structural self-sacrifice that, if unchecked, threaten both individual well-being and organizational sustainability. Recognizing this tension is critical for understanding the challenges SEs face and for designing policies and management practices that balance moral engagement with practical viability.

From a managerial and policy standpoint, these results suggest the need for frameworks that balance social mission and economic viability, promoting governance structures and incentive systems that support responsible agency, collective decision-making, and stakeholder participation. Integrating these principles could help SEs and other hybrid organizations become spaces for socially responsible innovation, fostering economic models in which social objectives and creative problem-solving are mutually reinforcing.

Based on Sen's understanding of economic agents and economic motives, future research and practical applications may further explore the interplay between commitment, self-sacrifice, and agency, particularly in contexts where social and financial objectives intersect. Extending the dualistic conception of the firm to other hybrid organizations (among others, B-Corps, worker cooperatives, or environmentally oriented SEs) could illuminate how ethical engagement and economic rationality coexist under different institutional and cultural conditions. Empirical studies could investigate how SEs operationalize commitment and social embeddedness across sectors and countries, particularly in relation to innovation dynamics and organizational performance. Comparative research may also examine the conditions under which commitment fosters sustainable social impact without leading to excessive self-sacrifice, thereby preserving both individual well-being and organizational resilience.

For all these reasons, our analysis reinforces the importance of recovering the social dimension in economic theory and practice. By reconstructing Sen's systematic approach to economic agents, we have shown that sociality, ethical dimension, and a plurality of motives are foundational to understanding economic behavior. The "Senian" perspective adopted to describe economic agents (both individuals and SEs) does not replace mainstream economic models but offers complementary insights into how ethical engagement, social embeddedness, and multiple motives operate in practice. In this sense, economic behavior cannot be fully understood without recognizing that responsibility towards others is not an external constraint, but an intrinsic component of decision-making itself.

Any account of economic behavior that neglects the social nature of economic agents, such as agency, commitment (even self-sacrifice), embeddedness, and responsibility towards others, remains fundamentally incomplete.

Index